Praise for *Losing Control, Finding Serenity*

"I found *Losing Control Finding Serenity* to be invaluable. I feel enriched by the many illustrative anecdotes and practical tips for letting go (in a mature and responsible manner) of the urge to control every aspect of my life."
—Mark Frauenfelder, Founder of Boing Boing

"Daniel Miller has hit the nail on the head with his hugely insightful book. As a parent and parenting author, I was especially struck by his chapter on losing parental control."
—Jennifer Worley, coauthor of *The Stay-at-Home Martyr*

"*Losing Control, Finding Serenity* . . . is must reading for all Type A workaholics. Through the clever use of well-positioned anecdotes, Danny Miller takes aim at the notion that to be successful in life, one must always be in control. I only wish that this book had been written forty years ago."
—Michael Sherman, founder of Delphi Information Sciences Corporation

"In my career as a professional writer and producer, I have spent over twenty years chasing those all-too-rare moments when the work almost magically flows to the page. In *Losing Control, Finding Serenity*, Danny Miller has homed in on how to achieve those moments by letting the creative process unfold naturally."
—David Krinsky, Executive Producer, *King of the Hill*, *The Goode Family*, and *Extract*, and writer, *Blades of Glory*

"*Losing Control, Finding Serenity* offers excellent insight and direction on how to let go of control at work and allow processes to unfold naturally, leading not only to better results but to greater serenity even throughout the most stressful situations. Indeed, anyone seeking to address issues with control can gain much from Danny's book."

—Marcia S. Ross, Executive Vice President, Casting,
Walt Disney Studios Motion Pictures Production

"*Losing Control, Finding Serenity* is a wonderful primer on how *not* to be judgmental of others so as to allow for them to fully actualize their own unique spiritual path. The fundamental 'decontrol precepts' that Danny Miller explains will enable clergy and laity to live more peacefully with themselves and their faith communities."

—James Lee Kaufman, Rabbi Emeritus,
Temple Beth Hillel

"Miller's insight into letting go allows people to become truly who God intends them to be and therefore more fully human."

—Rev. Canon Norman S. Hull

"Miller's simple methods help us lose the control that we think we need and gain abundantly more in our lives just by making a few 'decontrol' adjustments."

—Maria Carter, bestselling author of
Fall in Love with Your Life

LOSING CONTROL, FINDING SERENITY

LOSING CONTROL, FINDING SERENITY

How the Need to Control Hurts Us
And How to Let It Go

Daniel A. Miller

Ebb and Flow Press
Sherman Oaks, California

Caveat: Except for my own personal stories, the names and details in the stories have been changed to preserve confidentiality.

Although some of the concepts discussed in this book are derived from 12 Step programs, none of the material in this book has been reviewed, approved, or endorsed by any 12 Step program.

Published by
Ebb and Flow Press
13547 Ventura Blvd., # 93
Sherman Oaks, California 91423

Printed in the United States of America

Miller, Daniel Aron, 1943-
Losing control, finding serenity : how the need to control hurts us and how to let it go / Daniel A. Miller.
p. cm.
ISBN 978-0-9828930-0-5
1. Control (Psychology). 2. Peace of mind. 3. Self-management (Psychology). 4. Choice (Psychology). 5. Conduct of life. 6. Self- improvement. 7. Self-actualization. 8. Mind and body. I. Title.

BF611.M54 2011
158.1—dc22   2010939942

First Edition
16 15 14 13 12 11   10 9 8 7 6 5 4 3 2 1

Text and cover design by Bookwrights

To my wonderful children, Brandon, Lora, and Lana, who bring me great joy; my warm, loving wife and sweetheart, Sigute; my dear parents, Morry and Judy, whom I am blessed to still have in my life; and my caring sister, Suzee.

Control a. to exercise restraining or directing influence over: REGULATE b. to have power over: RULE c. to reduce the incidence or severity of especially innocuous levels <*control a disease*>

—*www.merriam-webster.com*

CONTENTS

There is a guidance for each of us, and by lowly listening we shall hear the right word.... Place yourself in the middle of the stream of power and wisdom which flows into you as life...then you are without effort impelled to truth, to right and a perfect contentment.

—*Ralph Waldo Emerson, "Spiritual Laws," 1841*

MY JOURNEY FROM CONTROL TO SERENITY

I WAS ALWAYS A CONTROLLER—I worried too much not to be. I firmly believed the best way to satisfy my needs and achieve what I wanted in life was by controlling everything and everyone. I constantly directed, pressed, persisted, advised, and tried to change others, particularly those closest to me. I hovered over everyone at work. Everything had to pass my close scrutiny and be done my way. At home, Father truly knew best! I advised my children on how to study, as well as how to interact with their friends. I also expounded on how they should play basketball, soccer, and tennis. And of course, in my infinite wisdom I was the one to make the "correct" decisions on important issues my present and former wives faced. In short, my way was the best way—and usually the only way.

Yet, by most standards I had a good life. I graduated from a top college and law school with high honors. I wrote a best-selling book on real estate investing. I developed and taught college-level real estate courses and conducted scores of seminars for real estate professionals throughout California. I also owned a real estate investment company that had well-known celebrities as clients. And by the time I was in my early thirties, I could afford to live in the exclusive Old Bel Air section of Los Angeles, next door to Sylvester Stallone and only a few doors down from where Elvis Presley once resided.

When I look back on it all, I see that my successes were less a function of my controlling ways than of the sheer time and energy I was expending. My workday didn't end when the sun set. I was driven. My mind worked through the night. Worry, anxiety, and fear were my constant companions, as they are for most controllers. I persisted, even when it was clear that events were well beyond my power to influence or change. I expected my employees to perform beyond their skills and education. At home, I could not accept that my children were different from me. I pressured my older daughter, Lora, to participate more in class discussions and school events when she had a social phobia. I scolded my younger daughter, Lana, for bouncing around so much when she was in fact bravely coping with tics from Tourette's syndrome. Indeed, I took everyone to task.

I thought things were fine, until one day they weren't.

EVENTS BEYOND MY CONTROL

A series of rapid-fire traumatic events in my late thirties shook me to my core. It all started with the unusually bad weather in Los Angeles during the winter of 1981. Eight straight days of heavy rains caused a major mudslide at our hillside home. I woke up early one morning, walked into the dining room, and looked out at our newly redesigned fifty-foot deck dangling halfway down the hill, precariously close to a neighbor's house. At first I thought I was sleep-walking. But after I showered and had three cups of coffee, the deck was still dangling. The repair costs almost equaled the price I paid for the home.

Weeks later, a mentally disturbed neighbor set a fire in my garage, directly below my eight-year-old son Brandon's bedroom. He had ignited a can of gasoline two feet from my car. (This neighbor was subsequently prosecuted for manslaughter when a person was killed in a fire he had set to an apartment building to collect insurance monies.) The fire singed my car and came within an inch of the gas cap before I doused it, barely averting a total disaster.

The incident so unnerved my first wife that she began sleeping in our son's room. (Little did I realize then that we would never sleep together again.) We installed sophisti-cated burglar and fire alarm systems and, for added mea-sure, bought a police-trained guard dog. We even purchased (and learned how to use) handguns.

We did everything we could but move out of the house. We couldn't do that because we couldn't sell it! There was still mudslide damage to be repaired, and we didn't have the funds to complete it. Plus, there was no longer vehicu-lar access to our home. That same neighbor had illegally graded his lot, cascading rocks and loose soil onto the foot of our driveway.

Soon afterward, I was betrayed by a business partner intent on squeezing me out of my most profitable invest-ment. He controlled the purse strings and began withhold-ing my badly needed profits from the investment. He also told my banker that my wife and I were unstable and that our finances had deteriorated. The problem was, we shared the same banker—my partner had introduced us—and my partner happened to be one of the bank's wealthiest clients.

The bank called in my loans—well in excess of $1 million in today's dollars—and I didn't have the means to repay them. A stable banking relationship was critical to my business. The sudden deterioration of my financial condition forced me to withdraw from pending real estate deals, wiping out more than two years' income.

Consumed with unbridled anger and resentment, I foolishly launched a costly five-year legal battle that brought me to the brink of bankruptcy. I was obsessed with revenge and with the foolhardy and impossible task of trying to make an honest man out of a dishonest one, and I used every dollar and controlling means available to me in my efforts.

I became distraught and scared—really scared. I was unable to sleep most nights and had horrible nightmares. My wife grew depressed. We soon separated. Too many crazy things had happened within several short years that fourteen years of a good marriage could not overcome.

It was time to face up to the imbalance and emptiness that dominated my life, but there was more to come. During the next three months, one of my most successful investment properties was completely destroyed by fire, and another suffered three robberies, one of which culminated in the shootout death of the robber (and the ensuing front-page headlines). This was followed by a mass exodus of tenants and foreclosure proceedings by the lender.

Next, my dear, beloved grandmother died. She and my grandfather, who had previously passed away, had literally raised me during my formative years. And my son, Brandon, then age ten, bearing the hardships of divorce and the chaos that surrounded him, developed severe vocal and motor tics. It was deeply painful for me to see the diminished glow of such a charismatic and enthusiastic young child.

I badly needed to get away and gain some perspective, so I took Brandon on a week vacation to Club Med in Mexico. When we returned, I went to the hospital for what I was told would be a simple twenty-minute outpatient procedure to remove a skin cancer on my right nostril—something I had kept putting off while dealing with all my travails— and ended up on the table for over three hours, followed by three additional major surgeries over a six-week period to eradicate the cancerous tissue, which had spread through my face like the roots of a tree. I lost half my nose, and it took several more surgeries to reconstruct it. I am fine now, but as luck would have it, my insurance coverage was dropped after the first round of surgeries.

The very thing in my life that I had always felt most secure with—CONTROL—no longer worked. It was time to give it up. I had neither the strength nor the desire to go on fighting whatever demons were going to attack me next.

DECIDING TO SURRENDER

I "surrendered."

And with that surrender, my blinders fell away, new opportunities emerged, and I was able to glimpse a more serene way of life, one that eventually led to great financial success, artistic achievement, and the most important thing to me now: greater serenity than I could ever have imagined.

When I returned to work following my surgeries, I noticed something quite remarkable. My business had been functioning quite well—without my constant direction! To be sure, there were many things I had to catch up on, but few of my fears had come to pass. On the contrary, several important projects had achieved positive results, with little input from me!

This was a startling revelation. Could it be that I couldn't control people or the outcome of events as much as I had thought I could? In fact, was it possible that trying to control too much might produce effects opposite of what I wanted? Were some matters best left alone or left to proceed at their own pace?

I was certainly curious to find out. I began observing the ebb and flow of work life. I noticed that each issue or challenge had its own unique course and time span, much like the waves of the ocean. Sometimes a transaction would progress smoothly and in an orderly fashion, while at other times things would get bogged down. Some matters would become confusing and uncertain, without any apparent direction. After a while I began participating in this process, but in a noncontrolling manner. I tried to roll with the punches, to go with the ups and downs rather than try to direct or resist as I had in the past. I still remained alert as I waited for opportune times to assert myself and apply my talents, but my involvement grew gentler and less obtrusive. I stopped assuming that my way was the best way. I stopped being so quick to judge. I listened to others and allowed them more leeway. On the whole this took very little time or effort on my part: perhaps I would offer a suggestion at an appropriate moment or simply acknowledge the good work of others. Frequently it meant slowing down and backing off when I realized I was slipping back to pressing, or realizing that more time was needed for key issues to become clearer. It also involved trusting my intuition and instincts much more. I had always had them, of course, but I had been reluctant to trust them.

The results of doing business in this way were remarkable. Eventually I ended up spending only half as many hours working as I had in the past because I was able to avoid time-consuming diversions and focus on what was truly important. I often discovered innovative solutions to complex problems because I was open to new ideas. I was considerably more relaxed. I smiled more and frowned less. I made fewer mistakes and wiser decisions. That really paid off.

LOSING CONTROL IN
MY PERSONAL AFFAIRS

Giving up control in my personal affairs, however, was more difficult and took longer. In fact, it was not until my third marriage that I was truly able to give up control with my family. (Indeed, my still-controlling ways had contributed to the failure of a short-lived second marriage.) I started listening to my wife, Sigute, and my children, Brandon, then nineteen, and Lora, then five (Lana was still to come). I stopped criticizing their choices and telling them what I thought was best for them. I stopped "taking care" of them so much and instead allowed them the dignity (and the chance to gain the wisdom) of making their own mistakes. I also stopped trying to change my friends and began to appreciate and accept them for who and what they were. In general, I accepted life more on its own terms and let myself be guided by what felt right and natural rather than by fear and anxiety.

It was during this period that I began to give up long-held, self-serving myths about myself: I conceded that I didn't know it all. My way was seldom the best way. In fact, I wasn't the great problem solver that I had taken such great pride in being (and I was not nearly as humble as I had deceived myself into believing). Lastly, I recognized that each person has his or her own unique life journey, and it was not my role to obstruct that journey by trying to overly influence it, but rather to support it through love, understanding, and acceptance.

UNEXPECTED REWARDS

I found that the more I let go of control, the less I obsessed and worried. Conflicts diminished. Family bonds strengthened. Intimate relations became more intimate. Friendships improved and sometimes changed if they were unhealthy for me. Creative horizons expanded. Work became more productive and enjoyable. And I felt much more at peace. By letting go of control, I was able to get in touch with a natural rhythm that was truthful and nonconfrontational yet followed no set pattern—one that invariably bestowed great rewards.

My own life bears witness to the remarkable rewards that come from relinquishing control. I now have greater balance in my life because I have the time and peace of mind to enjoy the very things that my time- (and energy-) consuming controlling ways had prevented me from doing. I went from an uptight, control-driven attorney and businessman to a life-loving person who works less and earns more, an accomplished painter, a published poet, a mentor, a tournament-level tennis player, a happily married man, and the involved father of three wonderful children.

ABOUT THIS BOOK

This book began to take shape over more than twenty years ago, after I had settled my harrowing lawsuit and took some much-needed time off. I purchased my first computer and started writing in a free-flow manner. My goal was to make some sense of what I had gone through.

I wrote about issues that had deeply pervaded my life for so long, such as gripping fear, obsessive worrying, and unmitigated anger and rage. As I faced new challenges over the years, I kept writing. These writings served as a personal self-help guide. Increasingly, it became apparent to me that there existed an inverse correlation between the compulsion to control and inner peace and security.

It is thus my sincere hope that this book will pinpoint the dangers of excessive control and show you how to let go of it. Once you do, you are sure to enjoy the serenity that follows. I've tried to provide tools and strategies for losing control in such important areas of your life as family and parenting, work, love and romance, sports, and creative endeavors.

Many of these "decontrol" tools, as I call them, come from my personal experiences, and some were inspired by the wisdom people have shared with me at various meetings and workshops over the years. Teaching others about control has also taught me quite a bit, and in this book I include those lessons as well.

Some decontrol methods overlap, and others simply take different paths to the same destination. Some may work better for you than others. Use what you like and discard the rest. Modify them and devise your own as you see fit. What is required for success is that you be open-minded, make the commitment, and have the courage to change your deeply embedded control patterns.

If you follow this path, you, too, will learn that *losing* control (or decontrolling) bestows upon you—and those around you—freedom of choice and contentment. It nourishes your soul as you act and respond to life's challenges with a more generous spirit.

PART I

CONTROL AND ITS CONSEQUENCES

CHAPTER ONE

THE COMPULSION TO CONTROL

Everything is determined, the beginning as well as the end, by forces over which we have no control. It is determined for insects as well as for the stars. Human beings, vegetables or cosmic dust, we all dance to a mysterious tune, intoned in the distance by an invisible piper.

—*Albert Einstein, interview,*
The Saturday Evening Post, *October 26, 1929*

DARREN WAS THE OWNER of a well-known women's clothing manufacturing company in Los Angeles's Garment District. The garment industry, known for being highly competitive and rapidly changing, is filled with very driven and demanding owners. Darren fit the mold well. He was a hands-on operator who was involved in all aspects of the business, from design and pattern making to fitting, mass production, and finally sales. His standards were high, and what Darren wanted, Darren got. For many years, his company produced a successful midpriced women's line. More recently, however, sales began shifting over to competitors who also featured high-end lines. To combat this, Darren started a high-end women's line at his company and hired an up-and-coming new designer, Martina, to jump-start it.

Martina enthusiastically came up with some original design and fabric choices for the spring season, but Darren felt they were too radical. He looked at the recent garments of his competitors and pressured Martina to make changes to her designs so that the garments would be what he considered market appropriate. Martina incorporated his changes, but Darren still was not satisfied. He pressured her to make still more changes, and she began to feel stifled. Her designs lost much of their originality. Simply put, they were flat. But Darren liked them and brought them to the large industry sales shows. Not surprisingly, they sold poorly.

The following season was more of the same, except Darren was even more insistent in his input, and Martina lost her enthusiasm. She felt like an artist without an art. She finally told Darren she couldn't go on unless she had more creative freedom, but "free reign" was not in Darren's vocabulary. Martina left to work for another company that allowed her to be the final arbiter of her designs. The market received her garments with record orders. In fact, Martina soon became so well known that she was able to establish a line named after her, which she later sold to the company for a handsome sum.

SETTING LIMITS IS ONE THING, BUT...

Life without control in some form would create havoc. Rigid control procedures are essential in such areas as science, medicine, and manufacturing, which require high degrees of efficiency and safety. Most societal and institutional forms of control—laws, regulations, procedures, and the like—are also important for our overall well-being and safety. Similarly, in interpersonal settings such as the workplace, the home, and the classroom, appropriate levels of control are necessary to assure productivity, education, and safety.

But Darren's story and ones like it are typical for those of us who feel constant pressure to control all aspects of our lives. We take for granted that that's what we should be doing—what we *must* be doing to survive. This goes beyond setting limits and standards, and often we don't even realize how far beyond we take it. How often do we stop to question how our compulsion to control may be harming us, whether at home with our children and family, at work, in our friendships, or in our leisure activities? Darren certainly didn't.

Young or old, male or female, rich or poor, teacher or preacher—we all have the compulsion to control. Control is a deeply ingrained part of our human condition. Indeed, it underlies the entire fabric of society. Our workplaces are hotbeds for control as the "survival of the fittest" is played out through intimidation, deception, and the drive to get ahead at all costs. On the world stage, powerful nations control by imposing their values and forms of government on weaker nations. And, of course, war is all about control.

Social institutions of all kinds try to control. Religion is controlling when it tells us what and how we should believe, lest dire consequences come our way. The political arena is rife with control strategies. Misinformation about candidates is broadly disseminated to discredit them and change voters' minds. High-stakes bartering is employed to force through partisan legislation.

On the home front, we control our partners and family by telling them what they should do and criticizing their choices. We control our friends by trying to change them. We even control in love by lavishing gifts and doling out kind words to court favor, crying to churn a lover's heart, pushing "hot buttons" to punish, and calculating when and how to bring sexual pleasure to our mate.

The means of control are diverse. When we press our views or wheedle or pout to get favored treatment, we are controlling. When we judge, intimidate, and raise our voices, we are controlling. When we lay a guilt trip on others, we are controlling. We control physically as well: we shove to get a better place in line, spank to discipline, flash our eyes and clench our fists to unnerve.

But controlling conduct is not always assertive or overt. It is often subtle or seemingly passive. We do it when we repeat a suggestion or express our views more than once, when we prod, cajole, or advise, and when we withdraw from loved ones or play the victim or martyr. In fact, most actions we take—or don't take—are controlling in some way. It's just a matter of how, when, and how much.

When we are driven primarily by strong emotions such as fear, anxiety, anger, and insecurity, we try to control excessively. This is when we pressure and manipulate people and events to get what we want or need (or what we think we want or need) or to try to change people in ways that we believe will be better for them—or for us.

At bottom, excessive control represents our attempt to change another's very nature and spirit. But because another's true spirit cannot be changed—except by that person alone—our efforts to do so are not only fruitless, they are also harmful. It is not about the other person as much as it is about us and our unwillingness to accept life as it is.

LENNY NEEDS SHARON

Will changing those closest to you truly satisfy your needs? Lenny thought so. Lenny was an internist who had recently retired. He had always looked forward to the day when he wouldn't have to be at the office all day and on call in the evening. However, he soon discovered that he didn't know what to do with his newfound free time. He began watching a lot of television and toyed around with his stock investments on the computer, but soon he became restless. His wife, Sharon, was very active. She played tennis regularly, had lunch with her friends, babysat the grandchildren, and volunteered at her church three days a week.

Lenny felt that he would be much more content if he and Sharon spent more time together, and he proposed that they learn to play golf. At first Sharon was reluctant because of the time commitment. Lenny brushed aside her concern and talked about how great it would be to be out in nature, as well as the benefits of fresh air and exercise. Sharon agreed to give it a try. They took lessons from a golf pro at the local driving range. Because of her busy schedule, Sharon was content just hitting at the driving range. Lenny, however, pressured Sharon to go out on the course instead and surprised her by buying her a new set of clubs. They began playing golf once a week, but that wasn't enough for Lenny. He tried to get Sharon to play golf with him two or three times a week. This was too much for her. He kept pushing, she kept resisting. Finally, Sharon announced she was done playing golf!

Like many people, Lenny was compelled to control because he looked primarily to others for his own well-being. Such people believe that if they can somehow change those closest to them, their own problems will dissolve. They have little or no awareness that the roots of their dissatisfaction lie within themselves. So, Lenny's "void" remained—and was even made worse by a resentful mate. Rather than use control to find contentment, Lenny would have been much better served had he worked through his own core emotions; in his case, loneliness and feeling unproductive.

THE FOLLY OF CONTROL

Nature teaches us the folly of control. When you observe nature for any period of time—perhaps while sitting under a tree or at the ocean shore—you can sense the presence of a natural process or rhythm. You may notice it in the way leaves fall from a tree, gently floating down to form eloquent patterns on the grass, or in the way ocean waves build, crest, and change course in an endless variety of movements. At such moments, we sense that the life force or energy we are experiencing is unpredictable and unknowable yet has an innate and vast intelligence all its own, one well beyond our capacity to understand. We also realize that, as mysterious as this universal rhythm is, we are somehow an integral part of it.

Life is in a constant state of motion: fluid, shifting, changing, always moving. As such, it is impossible to hold on to it—and that is precisely what controlling actions attempt to do. The result is much the same as if you tried to grab on to a rapidly moving conveyor belt, for example; you may slow it down momentarily, but you would ultimately get burned or dragged along! Consequently, when we control excessively, we are attempting to alter life's moving currents and rhythm. When we do this, we are unable to see options and make choices that would significantly improve our lives emotionally, spiritually, creatively, and financially. We become imprisoned by our fear, anger, and resentment and thus are not open to the wonders that await us. We also don't allow others their freedom of choice and the freedom to follow their life path, refusing to accept them for who and what they are and thus damaging close relationships.

We also worry incessantly. It is no accident that compulsive controllers have deeper frown lines than laugh lines. Most are obsessive worriers. They are preoccupied with "What if?" and "What might happen?" and "What should I have done?" and therefore miss the unplanned moments in life that are so special. Also, deep down, controllers know they really cannot control most things, and they obsess about that as well. Just reflect on the occasions when you worried and fretted about "pressing concerns" that never came to pass, at least in the manner and severity in which you had imagined. You probably would agree that in almost every instance you expended an inordinate amount of mental energy that had absolutely no impact on the outcome. But it did have an impact on your serenity!

This is why controllers have only fleeting moments of balance and tranquillity in their lives. Even then, these are moments that mainly tease rather than enrich because controllers must be alert at all times—sometimes even in the middle of the night. Controllers rarely relax. They can never afford to drop their guard, for who knows what awful demons might be lurking out there. What many of us don't realize is that the "demons" are actually inside us in the form of unprocessed, unwanted feelings such as fear and anger. The successes we do achieve through control never feel as good as they should and leave us craving the ever-elusive goal of fulfillment even more ardently. Even when our mission is accomplished, there still remains an internal emptiness. So we control again and again, only to find conflict and turmoil instead of peace and tranquillity.

In short, control deprives us of our serenity.

But you don't have to take my word for it. Consider the results and consequences of the occasions in which you were excessively controlling. Say, for example, you pressured your mate or a friend into doing something he or she didn't want to do. Or you were insistent that things be done your way. Or you hovered over someone at work to make sure the work was done the way you wanted it done. Or you resisted facing adversities concerning finances, relationships, events, and the like. I believe you will find that many of the control stories (mine and others) that I have included in this book are your stories as well.

WHY WE CONTROL

Many of us have almost no awareness of how often we control and how many ways we try to do it. Our very intensity and insecurity obscures awareness. Others, however, readily admit their malady. Some even take pride in calling themselves control freaks, although they may say they wish they could change their ways but don't know how or are afraid to try.

Why is it that people are compelled to control so much? Most of the time it is because we believe it works. We think we need to control people and events in order to get what we want. This is not unexpected. We are raised with control; it is taught to us and is all around us. Parents, bosses, teachers—much of what they do is control based. As young children, we grew up with controlling parents, but we learned from that and turned the tables by using unabated crying and temper tantrums to get our way.

Indeed, control is so deeply embedded in our social, economic, familial—and, unfortunately, moral—fabric that aggressiveness and intimidation are too often perceived as "values" to be admired. Consequently, if all we've ever known and felt comfortable with is control, we're bound to feel insecure without it. We may find it almost impossible to imagine a better and more peaceful way. Most controllers strive to attain, by whatever controlling means available, the external wealth and comforts that they believe will bring them happiness and security. The idea of giving that up is inconceivable.

But controllers are mistaken. However much they struggle, peace and security always remain just beyond their grasp. They can't quite get there, though it isn't for lack of trying. This spiritual hunger compels them to press harder and hold on tighter. They don't realize the inherent contradiction—that, as the philosopher Alan W. Watts explains in his book *The Wisdom of Insecurity* (Vintage Books, 1951), you can't hold on to something that isn't there:

> It must be obvious, from the start, that there is a contradiction in wanting to be perfectly secure in a universe whose very nature is momentariness and fluidity.... If I want to be secure, that is, protected from the flux of life, I am wanting to be separate from life. Yet it is this very sense of separateness which makes me feel insecure....
>
> To put it still more plainly: the desire for security and the feeling of insecurity are the same thing. To hold your breath is to lose your breath. A society based on the quest for security is nothing but a breath-retention contest in which everyone is as taut as a drum and as purple as a beet. (pp. 77–78)

Another reason why some people control so much is because their lives are unmanageable and "out of control." These typically are the people who suffer from addictions and emotional disorders (alcohol, drugs, rage, etc.) and the friends and families who care for them. The former feel compelled to hold on tightly for dear life to achieve some semblance of structure and stability in their lives; the latter are driven to take care of these victims by applying a wide array of control devices (enabling, assuming responsibilities, threatening, etc.). A common example is the wife of an alcoholic husband (or the husband of an alcoholic wife) who tries to "control" his drinking by scouring the home for liquor bottles and emptying them into the sink, then scolding him, pleading with him, and even threatening to leave him. Unless the husband is ready and willing to stop drinking, her forceful actions will only lead to heated arguments and sometimes even violence, as both parties fiercely try to impose their will on each other. Lives often spin out of control, causing immense suffering for everyone, including innocent children.

Some controllers, courageous enough to seek recovery through participation in 12 Step programs, soon learn that control is not the solution, and that only by giving up control can you gain control of your life. They learn how to give up control through loving detachment, wherein one party disengages from the conflict and focuses on the steps he or she can take to improve his or her own life. Rather than fueling the fire, they allow the fire to burn out by itself.

THE NEED FOR SELF-VALIDATION

Some individuals employ control as a means of self-validation. If I tell you what is best for you or what you should do, and you do it, you are validating me. The more I tell you what to do, and the more you do it, the more you will look to me—and need me—for further counsel. My sense of self-worth may increase, but at the cost of yours. If this continues, I will eventually become your enabler, and you my addict. This control dynamic is prevalent in parent/child and mate/mate relationships explored in chapters 9 and 10.

REPRESSING OUR HEART WOUNDS

What's true of most controllers, however, is that they have closed their hearts to unwanted feelings and injuries (many from their past), such as fear, anger and resentment, rejection, shame, abandonment, and betrayal. These core "heart wounds," when not given the opportunity to be healed by the compassion and wisdom of the soul, fester and become entrapped within, creating emotional, physical, and spiritual dis-ease and manifesting themselves in destructive, control-driven behavior.

The most prevalent "unwanted"—and therefore repressed—feeling is fear. Controlling conduct is most often fear based and usually is deep rooted and primal. At the core, it is the very fear of death. Ernest Becker argues this persuasively in his Pulitzer Prize–winning book, *The Denial of Death* (Simon and Schuster, 1973), in which he states that it is our inability as human beings to face the very fear of death—and of life—that both determines and undermines our mental well-being. We are afraid of the unknown and what the future holds for us. We are afraid that we will not get what we want or need unless we control, so our fears completely overwhelm any trust we might have to let matters take their natural course. These fears in turn stoke our anxieties and worries, causing us to control even more. We become so engulfed in this self-generating abyss that serenity is far removed from us.

Control thus becomes the mechanism we use to mask or appease our fears because the prospect of confronting them directly is simply too frightening. But this dynamic is flawed. It is like sealing a container of acid with a paper lid; the acid easily eats through and wreaks havoc.

MAKING A CHANGE

Excessive control obstructs our vision, and we fail to see our options. Instead, we become immersed in our fears and worries. Our creativity is quelled before it can blossom. Our spirit is repressed before it can shine. We become harnessed by our own restrictions and forgo vital life opportunities.

In the simplest of terms, a control-driven life is a serenity-deprived life.

Consequently, if we want greater peace and tranquillity in our lives, we must learn to *lose* control. We must stop trying to control events and others. We are powerless over most people and things, and we need to recognize that and give it up.

The compulsion to control takes time to develop, and it will take time and patience to reduce it. You can rest assured, however, that a strong desire and a commitment to change go a long way. In the chapters that follow, I offer strategies and tools you can use to help make it happen.

CHAPTER TWO

REMOVING THE BLINDERS

The sun will set without thy assistance.

—*The Talmud*

I FIRST EXPERIENCED THE benefits of giving up control some years ago, shortly after I had formed an investment partnership to purchase the largest and most expensive office building I had ever owned. My investors included celebrities and financiers as well as my attorneys and accountants. I was very excited about the property's prospects. It seemed to have everything going for it—quality construction and design, solid tenants, and a good location. In fact, I proudly considered it my flagship property.

Soon after the purchase, however, I had my unexpected surgeries. By the time I returned to work, the commercial real estate market had started to fall and eventually entered a severe downturn. My partners and I found ourselves faced with increasing vacancies. I tried everything I could to find tenants: expensive promotions and advertising (including free trips to Hawaii for real estate agents who brought us tenants), refurbishment of the common areas, rent reductions, and so on. I even changed the building's name. Nothing worked. Still, as the financial losses mounted, I pressed on, trying desperately to find the "missing element" that would make success happen. We were on the verge of losing our entire investment.

One day I was talking with one of my partners, who said, "Maybe the building is really a heavy anchor that's weighing you down. Have you ever thought about unloading it so you can focus on your other properties?"

I was stunned. The truth and common sense of what he said were immediately apparent, but I had never considered it because I was so preoccupied with trying to "save" the investment. I then stopped "working" the property. I mentally let it go and focused on my other properties, which I had neglected because I was compulsively seeking a solution to a problem that wasn't ready to be solved. In other words, I gave up control—although I didn't think about it in those terms at the time.

A short time later, a solution emerged that I could never have foreseen. Two of my so-called passive partners offered to fly out with me to meet with the party who had sold the building to us (and who was also our lender). They negotiated a sale back to him at a price that recouped almost half of our investment. My decision to back off turned out to be one of the best decisions I ever made. As I put my time and energy into my other properties, within a couple of years their collective value appreciated so much that it made up for the loss on the flagship property many times over.

With this I discovered one of the first benefits of giving up control: it expands your vision. Once I removed the blinders, options appeared that had been invisible to me before. Since then, time and again in all aspects of my life, I've experienced the remarkable vision that comes from letting go of control.

A MINISTER GIVES UP CONTROL

Niles was the pastor of a small multicultural church. He was well liked by the members, who appreciated his warm and engaging nature. As church membership grew, Niles needed an assistant minister to help him develop the church's multicultural programs. He held a series of interviews and selected an Ugandan woman named Butta. Butta had come to America after enduring severe hardships in her country, including the loss of many family members. However, unlike Niles, Butta was a serious and shy person, and theologically very conservative. Yet, because of her deep spirituality and strength of character, Niles felt she was the right person to teach and preach.

Soon after Butta began ministering, Niles became very nervous. He received complaints from church members that she was not friendly and that her teaching was too conservative for them. They wanted someone more like him. Niles urged Butta to try to be more personal and less dogmatic, but that just wasn't who she was. Niles continued to tell her what to do, to no avail.

Then Niles reminded himself of the very reasons why he had hired Butta in the first place: she had demonstrated that she was a woman of great moral integrity and courage and had displayed immense strength and deep faith under life-threatening circumstances. She was the type of role model his church needed. Niles realized he had to stop trying to mold her into someone she was not just to please church members. He stopped trying to control her ministry and simply allowed Butta to develop in her own way.

Over time, Butta blossomed into a warm, caring minister who brought her own special gifts to the church. Her unique approach allowed her to reach many people in the community who were not otherwise served, and Niles and Butta's ministry flourished.

THE RHYTHM OF TRUTH

I am forever hearing similar stories from others that when they stopped pressing and backed off on important issues, positive things happened. A television comedy writer once shared with me that he had aggressively pursued a hot new series without getting any results. As soon as he discontinued his efforts, he received a call from a network (whose offices were just blocks away from his home) asking him to be the lead writer on a new show. He said it felt as though the opportunity had just fallen into his lap.

I firmly believe there are reasons for these types of occurrences. The dynamic is akin to removing a barrier that has allowed water to pool in a garden bed. Water freely flows in diverse and unplanned routes throughout the bed, some paths twisting, others moving forward, some abruptly stopping, others splitting off in multiple new directions—but all flowing naturally. Without removing the barrier (i.e., relinquishing control), none of these diverse paths of opportunity would have appeared.

There is a natural flow, or energy force of life—I like to refer to it as the "rhythm of truth," or life's natural currents—that is intrinsically truthful and cannot be controlled or manipulated. It just "is" and, though ancient, is always "now." Within this rhythm of truth lie innate wisdom and inner peace and the solutions to many of our most challenging issues. I have learned that the more I am able to live my life in accordance with the currents of this rhythm, the more peace and serenity I am blessed with.

Removing the restraints is the key to accessing this rhythm. Releasing control frees the currents and offers us the opportunity to glide intuitively, creatively, and spiritually within them. It lets us establish and follow a personal flow that dramatically reduces the conflict, anxiety, and turbulence in our lives. When we are able to let go, new opportunities unfold—maybe not right away or as quickly as we would like, but at some point. As events and circumstances evolve, fresh ideas and choices appear, some almost magically.

TAKING CONTROL OF YOUR LIFE

I want to emphasize that *losing* control does not mean totally relegating your skills and talents to others or being unprepared to handle important tasks. Further, it does not mean reducing your leadership or sense of responsibility or adapting a laissez-faire, carefree attitude in which you let the cards fall where they may. Rather, it is a highly effective way of reorienting and applying your intuition, skills, talents—and grace—to a time and place in which circumstances are better aligned with your true needs and desires. Indeed, contrary to giving control of your life to others, letting go of control is instrumental in taking control of your own life. When the focus is off others, you can better take care of your own needs and improve your own shortcomings. Hence, to *lose* control is to *gain* control. You will also discover that a great weight has been removed from your shoulders because you are no longer as responsible for outcomes and results as before.

PART II

LOSING CONTROL

CHAPTER THREE

TAKING THE FIRST STEPS

Flow with whatever is happening and let your mind be free. Stay centered by accepting whatever you are doing. This is the ultimate.

—*Chuang Tzu, Chinese philosopher (369–286 BCE)*

NORMA CONSTANTLY WORRIED. She worried that her children were not doing well enough in school to get into a good college. She worried that her aging parents were not taking their medication. She worried about her overweight husband's high cholesterol count. The only way Norma knew how to soothe her worries was to take on the role of family taskmaster. She chided her husband for not taking better care of himself, calling him irresponsible. She insisted that her children study longer and harder. She called her parents daily to remind them to take their medication.

The results were hardly encouraging. Her husband ate healthier food, but only for a few days after Norma confronted him, and then he went back to his old eating patterns. Her parents promised they would take their medication but often forgot. Her children resisted studying harder, telling Norma, "We have a life, too!"

Yet, if you were to ask Norma if she considered herself a controller, she would look at you with a puzzled face and say something like, "What do you mean?"

ARE YOU A CONTROLLER?

Do your best to answer the following questions truthfully. Do you believe:

* Helping to remove your mate's clutter will result in her or him being neater?
* Searching for the "right" person will help you find the person who is right for you?
* Trying to perfect your work of art will make it better?
* Insisting that your daughter study for her tests without playing loud music will result in her getting better grades?
* Admonishing another person's rude behavior will make him act nicer?
* Repeatedly suggesting to a friend that she should ask her boss for a raise will result in her asking for one?
* Telling your sister that she needs to eat healthier food will result in her changing her diet?
* Telling your son how he should run his business will result in his following your advice?
* Harping at your husband about his excessive drinking will make him drink less?
* Yelling at your twelve-year-old son to be more aggressive on the soccer field will result in his playing more aggressively?

* Telling your golf partner that he needs to relax more when hitting his iron shots will result in his making better shots?

A predisposition to answer yes to more than a few of these questions is a good indication that you are a controller. Now, here's another question for you: even if you *don't* believe these things, do you still do them?

GAINING AWARENESS OF YOUR CONTROLLING WAYS

The first step in letting go of control is to become better aware of your controlling ways. Many of us have little inkling about how much, how often, and in what ways we try to control people and things around us. We can see it in others, but not in ourselves. (Try to control a controller, and you will see what I mean.) Quite a few, in fact, will deny it, so deeply ingrained are our control patterns. We are steadfast in our beliefs that our "good" intentions justify our constant efforts to "help" others see the light.

How does awareness start? It starts with an *honest* inventory of your control patterns. To do this, you have to reign in your ego and muster the courage to see yourself as you truly are—blemishes and all. For example, are you pushy? Aggressive? Demanding? Opinionated? Intolerant? Critical? Impatient? These traits are invariably intertwined with controlling behavior. Remember that self-justification and playing the victim are popular forms of denial. They are simply excuses for not owning up to your controlling role in your life drama.

Remember, too, that control is often subtle. Suggesting or reminding too frequently, encouraging too strongly, or preaching too intently are common control devices. Enabling others is also controlling. For example, when you repeatedly come to your children's "rescue," you are controlling. You are shielding them from life's challenges, which in turn deprives them of the wisdom and experience they would gain from having to deal with their own struggles.

You can also glean some insights into your controlling patterns by taking account of how others respond to you. What follows when you pressure your mate to do things he or she doesn't want to do? Or when you pressure your child into playing a sport he doesn't like? Or when you constantly try to do things for others that they should be doing for themselves? And if you are prone to conflict, it is important to assess what your role is in the "collision"—and whether you are controlling—rather than conclude that you were not at fault. There are very few, if any, incidents in which we do not play a part in the breakdown, but it takes self-honesty to own up to the fact.

If you do an earnest accounting of your ways, your control patterns will become more clear, and as mentioned before, awareness alone will make you control less. It is also useful to observe the controlling patterns of others in diverse settings—at work, in social gatherings, with family, and so forth. Observe, for example, what ensues when people persist or press their agenda too strongly, or when they are inflexible and closed-minded. Note the response when a parent uses an overbearing manner to tell his child what is best for her or what she should do, instead of simply listening to the child's concerns and apprehensions. Or see what happens when one spouse criticizes the choices of the other. Such controlling actions breed resentment, diminish trust, and discourage open communication between parties.

Conversely, observe the dynamics when people are accepting of each other—when they express their feelings, not their expectations, and when they listen attentively without trying to provide solutions. You will find more open communication and more intimate bonds because others feel safer in sharing their feelings and views.

GIVING UP CONTROL

There are many ways of giving up control. Here are just a few: When you walk away from an argument, you are relinquishing control. When you listen without trying to persuade or advise, you are giving up control. When you allow co-workers more input, you are letting go of control. When you pass the ball in soccer, you are giving up control. When you stop telling your spouse how to dress, you are releasing control. You are also *losing* control when you surrender or defer to others and back off—and sometimes simply do nothing.

LETTING GO OF CONTROL GRADUALLY

Once you've decided to try letting go, take care not to become obsessed with doing it. Gradual but steady is the best way. Giving up too much control at once is like removing a dam that holds back a large body of water. You'll experience massive (emotional) flooding. Good progress can be made by starting with a basic awareness of your controlling ways and with the desire, courage, and *patience* to change them.

A FRESH START

Once you have a clearer understanding of your controlling patterns, you can begin to take steps to let them go. The power of intention is highly effective in learning to let go of control. Start each morning with a decontrol affirmation. Here are a few to try:

- "Today I will not resist or persist."
- "Today I will accept others for who they are."
- "Patience is a virtue."
- "Today I will just observe and listen."
- "Today I will trust that everything will work out well."
- "Today I will accept things as they are."
- "Today I will be aware of the beauty all around me."

I recommend affirmations that personally speak to you. These will allow you to start your day more serenely. If you encounter difficult moments during the day, repeat your affirmations to get you back on track.

VERBAL DECONTROL CUES

Short verbal cues are another effective way of relinquishing control. When you are faced with an issue and feel as if you are at an impasse, try saying "Release it," "Let it go," or "Just surrender to it." Use cues that personally speak to you. These simple reminders quickly cut through the control urge by changing your focus and intensity. Later, when you revisit the issue, you may find that circumstances have changed.

As simple as these reminders are, however, we can easily "forget" to think about them while in the midst of our daily travails. It can be helpful to write them down and post them where you can readily see them, for example, on your desk, on the dashboard of your car, or by the telephone.

LOWERING YOUR EXPECTATIONS

High expectations fuel controlling actions. Expecting too much of others or of a situation leads to disappointment followed by control actions. An obvious example is when parents set too high of a standard for their children, be it in school, sports, performance, or the like. Setting reasonable, attainable goals goes a long way toward saving you and those around you from undue pressure, demands, and punishment.

Do not expect too much of yourself, either. When you do, you will start pressing and forcing the action, thereby disrupting the natural flow of events. Twelve Step programs have an apt expression in this regard: "It's progress, not perfection" that we should strive for. Hence, while it is perfectly acceptable to set goals for yourself, it is important that you pursue them in moderation and that they be realistic.

A FORTUNE COOKIE KNOWS BEST

I carry in my wallet a wise statement from a Chinese fortune cookie I opened many years ago. It reads, "You will find hidden treasures where least expected." Think about that for a moment. If you expect less, you control less—and find more. Conversely, when you expect more, you control more—and find less.

I have experienced this time and again. A good example is when I went to Lithuania on vacation with eleven members of my family. An avid tennis player, I brought all my tennis gear with high expectations of playing tennis during the trip. However, our group itinerary was extensive and I was unable to play for the first ten days. Each day I became progressively more irritable.

One morning it hit me that I was setting myself up for disappointment. I decided to totally release my expectations of playing tennis for the remainder of the trip. I affirmed that I would try my best to *lose* control for the entire day and just accept what came my way. Lo and behold, with no set "agenda," I ended up having the best day of my trip. I bicycled with my young daughter, Lana, through a beautiful forested park, and later swam in the Baltic Sea. It was a great day, and it was made even better when I received an unexpected call that evening from a local tennis player who contacted me through the hotel. He invited me to his club the next morning. Of course I accepted and had a blast playing tennis for the first time on red clay.

Be Humble

Attitudinal changes are instrumental in letting go of control, starting with having more humility. Arrogant and smug attitudes and thoughts such as *I know what's best, My way is the best way,* and *He's doing it all wrong* are ways of controlling. Who says you know what is best—particularly for others—or that your way is the best way? Only *you.* Changing such attitudes by being more open-minded, forgiving, and kind goes a long way in letting go of control. Be humble, and you won't stumble!

Changing Pace

In general, if you feel a loss of serenity, controlling behavior is likely involved, even though you may not be aware of it at the time. When this happens, change your pace or move on to something else. Go outside and breathe some fresh air. Read an interesting article. Do some journaling. Or just listen to music. When you "return," it is usually with a fresh perspective and a settled mind. For me, it helps when I visualize ocean waves and intuitively, almost viscerally, try to sense their ebb and flow. It's very calming, and that calm carries over to my day.

MAKE A MORNING COMMITMENT

Make this commitment to yourself: For the next week, when you wake up, you will have absolutely no expectations for the day—of others and of yourself, as well as of events—and see what happens. Tell yourself that you will take things as and when they come, that you will let the day unfold by itself. Commit to being open-minded, nonjudgmental, and accepting of others. Commit also to viewing obstacles or conflicts as opportunities for personal growth and not as forebearers of chaos and dis-ease.

I am confident that when you do this, your day will flow more smoothly. It may even hold a few pleasant surprises.

BE PATIENT

The de-control methods described in this chapter will set you on the path to *losing* more control in your life. However, be cognizant of the fact that while it is easy to *understand* the ways of giving up control, it is quite another thing to *do* them. Indeed, the transition from controller to relinquisher is not easy. For most, it will require changing deeply embedded patterns and ways. It is difficult for people who feel secure only through control—or, more accurately, insecure *without* it—to change gears. The fear of the unknown and unexpected is truly unsettling, particularly if you feel that you are relegating your well-being to others or to pure fate. Ongoing resistance—itself a form of control—is therefore to be expected during the transition. It is encouraging to know that there is always an important built-in safeguard: namely you. By that I mean there is an innate sense of self-preservation that will preclude you from leaving matters to whim and caprice. Initially, it is a matter of finding your own comfort level, and as you begin to experience the benefits of giving up control, it becomes more natural. Patience pays off.

CHAPTER FOUR

ACCEPTING "WHAT IS"

God grant me the serenity to accept the things I
  cannot change,
Courage to change the things I can,
And the wisdom to know the difference.

—*The Serenity Prayer*

WHEN I FIRST MET Anna, she was constantly being undermined by her mother, Emma, an only child who had im-
migrated to the United States from the "old country" after
World War II. Emma was ill-equipped to raise her five children in a culturally diverse country, and she made no bones
about not enjoying being a mom. Once she even told Anna
that if she could do it all over again, she would not have
had children. Nevertheless, Anna was a dutiful daughter
who dearly wanted a nurturing mother and thus continually looked to Emma for support and encouragement, but it
rarely came. Instead, Anna usually received criticism and
demeaning remarks from her mother. Yet, well into her
adult life, Anna persisted in seeking what her mother was
unable to give her and always got the same results.

Then one day Anna had an epiphany that dramatically changed the relationship between the two women. Anna had seen a movie in which the heroine was viciously attacked, and the first person she called for help was her mother. This made an impression on Anna. She realized that her own mother would have been the *last* person she would have called under similar circumstances. From that turning point, Anna began to accept her mother for who she was—and just as important, for who she wasn't! Because she did this, Anna also stopped trying to get from her mother that which could not be given. Interestingly, Anna and her mother's relationship improved dramatically. The control-like pressure was off Emma to be someone she wasn't. Over time, the two became friends and equals, and Emma began to open up more to her daughter. She even shared her feelings about growing older. When Emma later became gravely ill and was dying, Anna was there to share her mother's final intimate moments, in which they discussed the selection of songs and prayers, even the clothes and personal jewelry to be worn, at Emma's funeral. Thus, Anna's willingness to accept her mother as she was finally brought her the intimacy that she was unable to have by seeking it.

Acceptance Removes the Need to Control: The Serenity Prayer

The more we accept people and things for who and what they are, the less we need to control. True acceptance replaces the compulsion to change or control others and redirects our focus to where it should rightly be: on ourselves. In the process, this opens the door for significant personal growth and greater serenity. If you take only one thing away from this book, I hope it is this fundamental truth.

The degree to which you accept people, places, and things for who, what, and how they are is the degree to which you will have serenity in your life. The acceptance paradigm, "God grant me the serenity to accept the things I cannot change" is the very essence of the Serenity Prayer, which serves as the spiritual foundation of 12 Step programs.

The primary thing that we cannot change or control in any meaningful way is other people. All the effort and energy we expend in trying to do so, whether by reasoning, pleading, hoping, threatening, cajoling, or other controlling means, is for naught and at great cost to our own serenity. Others can and will change, if and when *they* choose.

This does not mean, however, that we should approve or condone how others choose to be or act; rather, we must accept that that is the way they are and it is not within our power to fundamentally change them. For example, we may strongly dislike, even disdain, certain traits of friends or mates, but if we constantly try to change them (by complaining or preaching, for example), it causes resentment.

Russ Wouldn't Change His Ways

A good case in point concerned Russ, a loyal, responsible, and trustworthy property manager who worked for me for many years. Russ had some very inefficient and annoying work habits that often resulted in careless mistakes and delays in completing important tasks. The crux of the problem was that Russ was disorganized and easily distracted. He was unable to set aside blocks of time in which to do his work. He insisted on answering every cell phone call that came in rather than letting them go to voice mail and returning the calls later. He also liked to visit with the tenants. Russ was the type of person that needed supervision but resisted it. I repeatedly asked him not to answer every phone call, and he would stop doing it for a while. I also asked him to write important things down on paper so he wouldn't forget, and he would do that for a while as well. But he invariably fell back into his old ways. Consequently, I would become very frustrated by the constant delays in completing his duties.

I realized that I essentially had two choices: replace Russ with someone else, or accept that I could not change his basic ways and try to adapt to them as best I could. I chose the latter. I concluded that his positive qualities were far greater than his shortcomings. After all, I, too, could be quite set in my ways, the difference being that I had the power to change and Russ didn't. I was grateful, however, for having a person on my team who was so loyal and honest, and whom our tenants appreciated.

Once I accepted these realities, my frustration lessened considerably and I was able to establish a work format that took better care of my needs. I hired part-time assistants when needed to help Russ complete important projects earlier. I also got more proactive. I spoke with Russ almost daily to get status updates and to review—and sometimes change—his work priorities.

A FRIENDSHIP NOT WORTH LOSING

Not accepting people for who they are can result in lost friendships. I once almost lost a longtime friend because I didn't accept his idiosyncrasies. Ethan was a rare individual who didn't have a cell phone or even an answering machine at home. The only way I could reach him was by leaving a message at his office. Consequently, he could get a hold of me whenever he wanted, but I rarely could do the same, particularly in the evenings and on weekends. I felt it was unfair and selfish of him. One day he remarked that he could always be reached, and I let him have it. I told him he was inconsiderate and that I resented his being so in control over when we could talk or make plans together. Needless to say, Ethan reacted angrily. I realized how childlike I had acted and apologized, but the damage had been done. We didn't speak for two years.

That incident brought home the fact that we are much better served by releasing our expectations of others, accepting them as they are, and examining instead the changes that we can make in our own roles in those relationships. Ethan's and my friendship resumed later, but on a different and, I believe, healthier basis. I was able to accept that he was very different from most people I knew and to release my expectations about when I might talk to him or see him. We saw each other much less frequently but still enjoyed each other's company. I am grateful that Ethan is a true friend who will always be there when I need him.

ACCEPTING THE CIRCUMSTANCES

There is a broad array of events and circumstances we clearly cannot change or control: computer glitches, traffic jams, power outages, flight cancellations, rained-out sports events, equipment breakdowns, bureaucratic inefficiencies, and the like. Even for a controller like myself, I was able to accept such adversities without much aggravation and move on because I was absolutely sure there was nothing I could do about them. My big problem lay with events and circumstances where I believed there was a small chance—even a minute one—that I could control the outcome. Sensing there was an opening, my controlling head would rear up in such forms as obsessing, pressing, and resisting. Inevitably those resulted in anxiety and frustration.

Fortunately, by then my acceptance threshold had moved forward considerably. And it continues to change because the process is ongoing. I now consider whether I can effectively change the circumstances, and if that is unlikely, I try my best to let it go. If I am unsure about something, I may try to influence events for a while to test the waters, but as soon as I feel discomfiting resistance or dis-ease, I move on.

CHANGING OURSELVES

The most important thing that we have the ability to change (or control) is OURSELVES. "Courage to change the things we can" includes our own shortcomings, attitudes, expectations, and reactions. In particular, we have the power to change our lives in profound ways if we acknowledge our shortcomings and try to improve them, rather than blaming others or making excuses for ourselves. However, to do so requires honesty in assessing our roles and our motives, which are woven into the fabric of our so-called grievances.

The 12 Step programs refer to this process as taking a fearless and searching moral inventory of ourselves. This truly can be a daunting task. It requires that we take responsibility for our "stuff," but it becomes much easier when we stop trying to control others. The next time, for example, that you become upset at someone for what he or she did or said, stop and ask yourself, What was my role in it? Do I bear any responsibility for what happened? If we are truthful with ourselves, in almost every instance we will find that we played some role in what happened. We may not have clearly communicated our feelings or desires to others. We may have had unreasonable expectations of others. We may have been smug or intolerant. Even if we played a minor role, it still impacts our serenity, and acknowledging that role reduces the discomfort.

THE WISDOM TO KNOW THE DIFFERENCE

It would be simple indeed if we could readily distinguish between what we do and do not have the power to change. In truth, however, the distinction is frequently difficult. Strong emotions—fear and anger, for example—as well as high expectations easily thwart even our intentions to realistically consider whether the issue is something over which we truly have control. Moreover, the line between wishful thinking (that we can control something) and reality is often blurred. On other occasions, we may be able to influence things only up to a certain point, and then we need to be wise enough to let go.

For many, the requisite wisdom comes only after painful personal experiences and mistakes. All too often I learned my lesson this way. One instance was the foolhardy battle I had with the powerful business partner I described in the introduction to this book. In the midst of gruesome litigation, I righteously announced to my attorney my intention to make my partner stop taking advantage of people and make an honest man of him. Dumbfounded, my attorney turned to me and exclaimed, "Danny, you must be kidding! Do you really think you're going to change this man? That's just not going to happen."

I was so consumed by anger that not once had I considered my efforts were doomed from the start.

BECOMING WISER

You might be asking this question: How can I learn to avoid doing this? Well, when faced with contentious issues, first consider whether you can realistically expect to change matters. If the answer is yes, next ask yourself whether any "success" is worth the cost and energy—and anguish. Fear and anger *will* raise their heads, and you must process that. Try neither to react impulsively nor to retaliate. (Chapter 5 offers effective ways of doing so.) In this manner, you can evaluate what is really at stake and assess how important it is in order to respond more calmly and realistically.

Sometimes it is better to surrender than to win. That does not mean you have given up or are submissive; rather, it means you overcame a wounded ego, accepted "what is," and devoted your energies to more positive things.

A case in point: another business partner of mine unilaterally changed the terms of our investment agreement to benefit himself financially. I was upset because it was presented to me as a fait accompli. When I first learned of it, I almost withdrew from the investment on the spot. However, having learned from the harmful consequences of my earlier impulsive conduct, I elected to step back and reflect on the matter for the next few days. By doing so I realized that my strong emotions had prevented me from seeing three important truths. One, I was powerless to change my partner's decision since I was a minority partner. Two, some of the changes would benefit me as well. Finally, the business opportunity was still very advantageous for me in its altered format. I was then able to let go of control by accepting "what was" and base my decision on facts rather than on emotions. And to my eventual surprise, my partner reversed his decision and returned to the terms of the original agreement—something I would never have achieved had I forced his hand.

Prayer and Meditation

"The wisdom to know the difference" is also frequently revealed through prayer and meditation. We can pray to God, a Divine Presence, or a Higher Power for the wisdom and guidance to make the right decision—for us. Similarly, we can meditate to clear our minds so that we can examine issues more calmly and objectively. Through such means, we gain clarity and perspective on troublesome issues, particularly where there is a fine line between what we can and cannot control, and we can better understand the likely consequences of our actions.

Ask yourself, Is this something I really have the power to change or control? How important is this to me? Is this something that is best left alone for now? Am I making a mountain of a molehill? Remember, not everything is a crisis, but anything can become one if you fail to *lose* some control.

Turning It Over to Our Higher Power

It can be extremely difficult when we get to the point at which we know we are powerless over a situation and need to let it go. We are only human, after all. We are never free from the perennial conflict between what we *know* to be true and how we *feel* about it. We often do not trust that things will work out if we leave well enough alone, or we fear that others will harm us. If you are having particular difficulty with this move, the 12 Step program's concept of a Higher Power can be of considerable comfort. If we can come to believe that there is (or may be) a power greater than ourselves—be it a Divine Presence, or God, as we understand him (or her); or nature, a transcendent energy force beyond our knowledge or ability to understand—we can then turn over to this Higher Power the things we cannot control. A shorthand phrase for this is "Let go and let God."

The concept of a Higher Power is very personal and individual and is often based on our own experiences, epiphanies, insights, and wonderments. For many, it is also based on religious beliefs. However, we need not be "religious" or follow an established religion in order to believe in a Higher Power. The idea of a Higher Power can be tailored to meet our personal comfort and acceptance level. We need only accept that there is a force, or "something," that is greater than ourselves, that we are not omnipotent or omniscient. The essential point is that if you are able to turn the things you cannot control over to "something" greater than yourself, then it is out of your hands, so to speak, and the compulsion to control diminishes considerably, and with that your obsessions and anxieties. You literally feel the burden lifted from your shoulders.

John Discovers His Power

Consider, too, that once you are at this point, you have viable options. Accepting "what is" forges its own paths. Take the case of John, who liked order and neatness in his household, and his wife, Gena, who was a clutterer. (Of course, the reverse is just as often true!) John constantly tried to get Gena to clear away the clutter. He complained and nagged, even pleaded. Gena paid lip service to him and removed some clutter, only to have it reappear several days later. John continued harping until Gena resentfully retorted, "You try taking care of the kids, doing the shopping, doing the laundry...*and* keeping the house neat!"

The end result was that John became enmeshed in turmoil by trying to control what was *beyond* his power to control. And for all his trouble, he still had to live with clutter. *Finding* serenity for John began with his *recognition* and *acceptance* that, as much as he may wish or try, Gena will not change unless (and until) she is willing or able to change. (Gena may in fact want to change but simply may not be able to.)

John, however, began to focus on the changes that *he* had the power to make in *his* ways and attitudes. For example, he obviously could remove the clutter himself, or he could secure his own separate "space" within the home and maintain it the way he liked. He also had the option of relieving his wife of some of her domestic responsibilities so that she had more time to tend to her own needs. (Note that this will not work if Gena is not ready to make the change herself.) Still another option was to enlist their children's help.

More important, on an internal level John reflected on why he was so impacted by clutter; in other words, he tried to ascertain what core emotions were stirred up for him and what needs of his were unfulfilled. Perhaps it was financial anxiety, work pressures, or just general malaise that made being around clutter unbearable for him. Addressing these issues, these important "truths," brought him some peace of mind. Eventually he got to the point where his wife's clutter no longer disturbed him as much!

JANICE FINDS HER POWER

Another case in point concerned Janice and Liz, two design partners who had vastly different work habits. Janice was a back-office manager who kept a neat desk and maintained complete and accurate files and records. Liz was a creative sort who brought in the business but hated paperwork (except on her desk, where it was mounted high!) and rarely took notes. When new clients were recruited, Janice prepared the retainer agreements and Liz sent them out under her signature. Sometimes, however, Liz modified the agreements without informing Janice and on occasion got distracted and misplaced them.

As one might imagine, Liz's carelessness unnerved Janice. Janice repeatedly reminded Liz about the importance of being better organized and keeping her informed. Liz tried but didn't (or couldn't) change her ways. Janice took all of this very personally—she didn't feel Liz was truly making an effort to change—and became angrier and angrier until she finally snapped at Liz. This did get Liz's attention, but now friction thickened the air.

Janice eventually realized that the only way she could avoid such angst was by no longer trying to change Liz's way of doing business. Instead, she began to consciously focus on changes that *she* had the power to make in *her* role in the business. She thus made it a habit to follow up with Liz often and ask for the status of their projects.

My point here is that each and every situation in which we find ourselves offers choices. However, to truly see them we need to stop trying to change others (and things), simply accept "what is," and think about what actions we have the power to take. No matter how great the challenge, once we honestly examine our own role in such situations and the changes we do have the power to make, viable options appear that will bring more serenity than we might think possible.

An Exercise in Discovering Your Power

To identify the issues in your life that are the most problematic and over which you feel powerless, I highly recommend the following exercise. First, on a sheet of paper, write down your issues. Include relationships (family, friends, co-workers, etc.) and situations or circumstances (health, work, finances, etc.) that stoke your fears, anxieties, and resentments. Leave a few inches of space between each listed item.

Next, consider where in each issue you do have power or control, and describe this in the spaces you provided. You will soon notice that even though you may feel powerless over certain aspects of a situation, you are not without options. This recognition alone can go a long way toward easing a sense of helplessness.

To demonstrate more specifically how this empowerment exercise works, let me share with you how I found my power with respect to my daughter Lora's enjoyment of tennis. I urged Lora to attend tennis clinics to hone her skills so that she would be able to play on her high school varsity tennis team. She attended a few clinics but disliked the extremely competitive atmosphere. I kept pushing her to continue, and she kept resisting. One time I was so persistent I brought her to tears. She told me she didn't want to play tennis anymore. I was crushed. I knew I had let my ego get in my way.

I took an accounting of my controlling ways with her and realized that the constant pressure had taken the fun out of the sport for her. First, I examined the issue (Lora's tennis) and considered what aspects of the issue I was powerless over. I concluded that I was powerless over her:

* Not fulfilling her potential
* Not enjoying competition
* Lacking confidence
* Making the varsity tennis team

I then considered where my power did lie with respect to her tennis. I concluded that I had the power to:

* Reign in my own ego
* Lower my expectations about her tennis
* Be supportive of Lora and whatever choices she made
* Enjoy just playing tennis with her
* Focus on improving my own game

What ensued was totally unexpected. Because I hadn't played tennis myself in over twenty years, I took lessons and thereafter joined a local tennis club. I made new friends and enjoyed playing much more than I had in the past. Moreover, my game progressively improved, and within two years I started entering seniors tournaments. Two years after that, I won my first tournament (men's doubles in the annual Los Angeles Metropolitan Tennis Championships), and successfully defended the title the following year.

Lora, of her own volition, tried out for her high school team. She played junior varsity doubles for two years and then varsity for two years; her varsity team won the Southern

California title in its division. Today Lora and I enjoy playing tennis together just for the fun of it!

MAKING THE BEST OUT OF DIVORCE

Knowing where your power lies is particularly helpful in highly divisive situations such as divorce and custody battles. A good example involved June and Gary, who were divorced (June had left Gary for another man) and shared custody of their young son, Michael. June felt that Gary constantly undermined her relationship with Michael by being critical of her in addition to being more lenient in raising Michael. In other words, he was the good guy and she the bad guy. Over time, June became more and more resentful. She began to retaliate in kind. This only led to greater upheaval and a worsening relationship with her son, who was caught in the middle of his parents' feuding. June finally meditated on what she could and could not effectively do with regard to the serious imbroglio, and concluded that she was powerless over:

- How Gary parented Michael
- Gary's taking the "moral high ground" all the time
- Gary's disparaging comments about her
- Gary's enmity toward her

June then considered what she did have the power to do. She concluded that she had the power to:

- Let go of her resentment of Gary and not retaliate in kind
- Try not to take things so personally
- Examine her own part and motives in the conflict and make appropriate changes

- Be compassionate about Gary's unhappiness
- Work on bettering her relationship with Michael

These types of exercises can serve as powerful healing tools, for they help to provide a more balanced perspective on a wide range of troublesome issues and challenges.

Most important, be constantly aware of the fact that you do have the power to change or control many things in your own life, including your attitudes, your expectations, your reactions, your intentions, and your commitment to improve your shortcomings. By exercising this power, you will make your life much more serene.

ONCE MORE, ACCEPTING "WHAT IS"

For us controllers, accepting "what is" represents a dramatic shift in thinking, believing, and acting. It requires considerable effort—and courage. Even partial success in accepting "what is" not only gives you more time and opportunity to pursue your interests and passions but also brings you greater serenity. For that reason alone it is worth trying, no matter how skeptical you may be.

EMBRACING YOUR
PERSONAL TRUTHS

Truth is Truth,
To the end of Reckoning.

—William Shakespeare,
Measure for Measure,
act 5, scene 1

PRIOR TO HER MARRIAGE, Marcia was a hardworking, successful magazine illustrator. She particularly enjoyed her financial independence, and in her own small way enjoyed being a philanthropist for her favorite causes. Marcia was thirty-five when she met Tom, a general contractor. After dating for a year, one day Marcia heard the proverbial ticking of her biological clock and exclaimed to Tom, "I want to have a baby!"

She and Tom soon married, and their first child, Jason, arrived a year later. Marcia began working only part-time so she could more fully enjoy motherhood, and when their daughter, Julia, was born, she stopped working altogether. Marcia felt guilty, however, that she no longer was able to contribute to the family finances. She wasn't used to not "paying her way." To compensate, she took on the role of homemaker extraordinaire. She kept the house spotless and in perfect order, cooked gourmet meals for the family, personally ironed her husband's dress shirts, and mowed the lawn and cleaned the pool to save money.

At the end of most days, Marcia was exhausted. Yet, she stoically endured her burdens, all the while resenting deep down that she had precious little time (or energy) for herself. She was very conflicted. She wanted—needed—help but felt bad asking for it. After all, Tom was the provider for the family. Not surprisingly, however, Marcia's resentment mounted and she became very controlling. She began ordering the children around and making snide comments to Tom about his puttering around the house and never lifting a finger to help.

By not addressing her guilt, resentment, and deprivation, Marcia created unnecessary family turmoil. Sadly, also, her eruptions failed to bring her the "relief" she so badly wanted.

EMBRACING OUR PERSONAL TRUTHS

Each day we experience a wide range of feelings that impact us emotionally, physically, and spiritually. These feelings are our intrinsic Personal Truths. They are the real us—our heart and soul—shed of all facades and defenses. They include our fears, resentments, anxieties, shame, sadness, insecurities, and the like, some of which may have dwelled deep within us for many years. When these "unwanted" Personal Truths are not processed, they fester within until they find external (and often destructive) outlets through controlling actions. That is to say, when we are "out of control" internally, we compensate by trying to control externally.

To avoid such trauma, it is necessary to find ways to process our unwanted feelings. Ironically, the best way to loosen their grip is to embrace them. By this I mean acknowledging and processing them—and not just in passing. They must be given their full due, regardless of how painful they are or how vulnerable acknowledging them makes you feel. They are part of the real you. Don't think of them as good, bad, or abnormal, but rather that they exist and need to be dealt with. They are feelings, not facts! Remember, they are not your core values and belief systems, although they can impact those systems.

Some of these uneasy feelings can actually result in positive changes in your life if they are addressed and redirected. For example, Marcia could have processed her frustration by having a heart-to-heart talk with Tom and letting him know the full extent of her workload and how weighed down she felt, and confessed her guilt over it. She could also have let Tom know that she felt deprived by not having the time and energy to pursue her own interests.

Such a discussion would likely accomplish several things. First, it would clearly communicate to Tom important information he might not have been aware of until he was "bludgeoned" by her pent-up resentment. It would also provide a constructive opportunity for him to assist Marcia, such as offering to carry more of the workload himself, or getting the children to help out, or even hiring help for her.

Opening our heart in this manner enables us to connect with our soul center, and it is from this centered core that we will feel not the compulsion to control but the strength to address life's challenges in a straightforward manner. And in the process you will defuse potential conflicts with grace as others instinctively accept the purity of your truths. In short, your spirit will shine!

MARILYN AND BILL: FACING THEIR FEARS

Embracing your Personal Truths is particularly helpful in divisive situations. Take the case of Marilyn and Bill's bitter divorce battle. The two had been married twelve years and had two children, ages eight and ten. Bill had a good job as vice president of a large outdoor-furniture chain. Marilyn was a stay-at-home mom, having given up a successful career as a graphic designer. When the battle began, Bill was afraid he would be "taken to the cleaners" by his wife and not remain an integral part of their children's lives. Marilyn had grave fears about her financial security and was bitter that she gave up "the best years" of her career.

Experience tells us—just ask anyone who has been through a nasty divorce—that if the core truths of the parties are not adequately addressed, they will obstruct the path that could lead to a fair resolution. Fear-based controlling conduct will be rife with threats, manipulation, deceit, and a rush to judgment. Scenarios of gloom and doom will prevail over reasoned consideration of salient facts and the best interests of the parties and their children. In short, only the attorneys will benefit.

Hope for a peaceful resolution in such cases lies with the parties being able to disengage and demonstrate the courage, humility, and utmost honesty to address their intrinsic truths, individually and together. Bill must get in touch with his fear and sadness of being alone and not being an integral part of his children's lives, and express those concerns to Marilyn. He should also share with Marilyn his fear of having to support two households. At the same time, however, Bill needs to acknowledge another important truth: that the well-being of his children must include taking into account the well-being of their mother, including her financial needs. Similarly, Marilyn needs to acknowledge the instrumental role that Bill has played in the development and well-being of their children and let Bill know of her desire for the children to spend meaningful time with their father. She should also convey to Bill her willingness to work toward a fair property settlement agreement.

The parties also need to accept "what is," and that includes the undeniable fact that their lives have changed in significant and challenging ways. Things won't and can't be the same as before, and that needs to be truly accepted by them so that they can move on with their lives in constructive new directions.

BECOMING AWARE OF YOUR PERSONAL TRUTHS

To embrace your Personal Truths, you first need to become aware of them. Awareness alone can be a highly healing presence. Readily identifying their intrinsic truths is second nature to only the relatively few. These fortunate individuals have a heightened sense of inner peace because they are genuinely accepting of themselves and others. They trust and have great faith that most things will work out well in their universe and thus have little compulsion to control. This enlightened class includes not only shamans, healers, spiritual leaders, and the like but also those who have made the commitment to become more aware of their feelings on a day-to-day basis.

For many of us, however, identifying our Personal Truths can be quite difficult. They are easily masked as we become engulfed in our daily storms. Too, some of us may view them as unsavory or abnormal and hence try to conceal them. For still others, the pain of their heart wounds obscures their true feelings.

To become aware of your Personal Truths, you need to repress the urge to quickly push through them. By that I mean you must stop and "listen" when you don't feel "right" or when things feel awry. Be observant of your discomforts, your anxieties, and your physical symptoms as they arise, even if you do not know what has caused them. Take a few breaths and try to get in touch with what is happening internally.

Listen to Your Gut

I can provide no better example of what I mean than the time I failed to listen to what my gut was trying to tell me during the final phases of writing this book. I had invited a diverse group of friends to a prepublication book salon in which I intended to discuss the primary ideas and concepts of this book publicly for the first time. Two weeks prior to the salon, I began to feel weak and had an upset stomach. I assumed that I had contracted a small virus. But when my intermittent stomach cramps lingered on for four or five days, I was concerned that I might be developing an ulcer. When I started getting cramps while I was at my daughter's volleyball game, I closed my eyes and felt a tightness in the pit of my stomach. I breathed deeply for a few minutes into the tightness and experienced what felt like an electric current—for me a telltale sign of fear's presence. I tried my best to "relax" into the current, and soon the tightness began to dissipate. I kept doing this, and it finally left altogether.

That evening I looked into what might have been bothering me, and I realized that I was fearful and anxious about promoting the book. The book salon would require me to come out of the "safe harbor" of writing. Now I would have to actively promote myself, expose my ideas, and test their merit. It was an amazing revelation for me—and just as amazing was the fact that my cramps did not return. That is because once I was aware of my fears, I took steps to address them.

BERNARD FAILS TO ADDRESS HIS FEARS

Another example of what can happen when you don't embrace your Personal Truths is when Bernard, a business acquaintance of mine, was confronted with an abrupt delay in the closing of an important business deal that he had been laboring on for over three months. His money source had had a change of heart at the last moment, and Bernard panicked. He quickly tried to salvage the deal by contacting other prospects, but his sense of urgency repelled them. Bernard became so frustrated and resentful that he called his original source and told him just how he felt. Not once did he stop to get in touch with the powerful and conflicting feelings that engulfed him: betrayal, resentment, and fear.

When Bernard related the story to me, I asked him what happened when he lashed out at his client. "He got so upset at me," Bernard said dejectedly, "that he told me to forget about considering him for future deals. I totally lost it and told him I didn't need him anyway. End of that relationship. I really felt undermined. But what could I have done about it?"

"You didn't honor your Personal Truths," I explained.

"What do you mean?" he asked.

"Well, what were your immediate feelings when you learned he was backing out of the deal?" I replied.

"Extreme disappointment. Fear and a lot of anger," Bernard answered.

"You needed to process those core feelings," I said.

"That all sounds well and fine, but that still doesn't tell me what I could have done differently," he snapped back.

"First," I said, "you should have acknowledged those feelings—really felt and stayed with them. They were very real and painful feelings and needed your attention. But you masked them and instead pressed hard to find a quick fix to your dilemma. By doing that, you were rude and abrasive and likely nipped possible options in the bud."

Bernard reflected on that for a moment. "You know, I think you are right. Do you think it is too late to rectify the situation?"

"It may be, but it's not too late to address your Personal Truths. What are you feeling at this moment?" I asked.

"Sadness, regret, and fear again," he responded.

"Let him know that," I suggested. "Apologize for your rudeness, and let him know how fearful you were. You can also let him know how much you value your relationship with him and that you sincerely hope he will consider your future investments."

Bernard eventually managed to restore his relationship with his client and closed several business deals with his support.

LEARNING TO EMBRACE YOUR PERSONAL TRUTHS

Once you are aware of your Personal Truths, you can embrace or process them, which is ultimately a personal exploration of ways that work best for you. There are no set rules. What works well for one person may not for another. The key, however, is to directly face these truths. Even making partial headway helps considerably. Below are some ways that have worked well for me and others I know. They are by no means exclusive and are not intended to limit your personal explorations and discoveries.

Faith is a powerful means for processing unwanted feelings. Hence, for many people, religion is instrumental in processing their Personal Truths, whether it be through traditional religious services and rituals, individual prayer, readings of holy books and scripture, or the support and counsel of religious leaders and others within a community.

Many people address their Personal Truths through such spiritual means as meditation, visualizations, and participation in 12 Step programs. Some simply take a few moments to reflect on the day or go for a walk. For others, listening to music or working on a creative project puts them in touch with their core feelings.

Journaling is yet another effective way to get in touch with your inner feelings. I prefer simple free-flow writing with little "thinking" involved. I just write whatever comes to mind; I try not to judge or analyze. Oftentimes wonderful insights unexpectedly spring forth.

Centering yourself through deep breathing exercises is an excellent way to process your unwanted feelings. These exercises are practical and convenient because they can be done almost anywhere and don't require much time. They can be done sitting or lying down. One method involves inhaling slowly through your nose for five counts (or more), holding your breath for five counts, and then slowly exhaling through your nose for five counts. It is important to breathe into your abdominal area. After a few minutes, you will experience a soothing calmness and relaxation as you become centered. Your thoughts become more clear as your inner truths reveal themselves.

Taking it a step further is an exercise in which you focus on the area just below your navel as you breathe slowly. After a few minutes, you should start to feel a physical sensation—for me it is a tingly sensation, like an electric current. These sensations emanate from the abdominal area to other parts of your body and typically encompass your fears and anxieties. When you are able to stay with and relax into these energy currents, your anxiety lessens and you become very aware and in the moment.

Similarly, many people utilize mind-body practices whose common theme is that the body is impacted by our emotions and life experiences. When we release, or "free," our body, our emotional truths are also released. Yoga is a highly popular example. When you control, your muscles constrict. Through the combination of proper breathing and specific body positions and stretches (called asanas), the practice of yoga teaches you how to release, both mentally and physically. Deep relaxation and connection with your inner self result. Indeed, yoga's very essence is losing control through surrendering.

Embracing your Personal Truths also includes getting in touch with your physical being. By that I mean feeling and acknowledging your body's pains and discomforts. Think of this as physical centering. Your body is impacted by your daily travails as much as your mind is; you may just not be aware of it. We typically complain about that dreadful headache, as if our head were not part of our body. But our connective tissue and nerves do not end at our neck. They extend well into our head.

Physical exercise of all forms is thus very helpful. Master swimmers who swim intensive sets of several miles at a time say that swimming is a form of meditation for them. Runners report the same experience. I have found that even doing simple stretches works well. Almost anything that releases muscle tightness brings clarity of mind. When you are physically fit, the mind follows. That is why whenever I have to deal with critical life challenges—whether personal or business—I resort first to strengthening my body. I took karate lessons for several years to help me deal with my extreme anxiety during my battle with my former business partner.

If I had to pinpoint what seems to me inherent in all these practices, it is the fostering of stillness that calms our mind, relaxes our body, and allows us to be in the present. I refer to this grounded state as Truth Centering because it is from within this centered core that our Personal Truths are revealed and processed by us.

PROCESSING THROUGH DAILY PRACTICE

As mentioned earlier, awareness of your Personal Truths is extremely important. With awareness comes action. We tend to bury our truths inside because they're often too painful to face. That is why it is important to find ways to keep them on the surface as much as possible. Here are some effective daily practices that will allow you to quickly identify and process your Personal Truths.

First, start your day with a ten-minute centering exercise—a short meditation, prayer, or journaling, for example—and repeat with shorter ones as the need arises during the course of the day. When you start your day centered, it is much easier to restore that state later.

Second, try not to rush through the day. When you do, you "pass" your feelings and thus disconnect with your inner reality. Take some time-outs to breathe, reflect, or meditate so that your feelings can "catch up" with you. Allow the union of your feelings and actions to replace your disconnect and anxiety.

Next, when you encounter conflict or dis-ease, do not act or react right away. Take some time to get in touch with what has happened and how you were impacted by it. Consider whether you had a role in the issue and whether you made assumptions without knowing all the facts. Then respond in a manner that addresses these truths. For example, if your feelings were hurt by what someone said or did, express the hurt rather than withdraw or lash out in anger. Anger is a control response, whereas expressing your true feelings is a healing response, and one that may open the door to meaningful resolution.

Finally, make sure you honor your physical being during the day. Listen to its innate wisdom and let it be your guide. When you feel physical discomfort or pain, take some time to get in touch with it. A stiff back or headache may be a symptom of a strong emotion or feeling that has not been acknowledged. When your head feels tight, give yourself a "brain massage" by massaging your scalp, temples, and face.

SYNERGISTIC INTERPLAY

In practice, embracing your Personal Truths and relinquishing control go hand in hand. When you relinquish control, you are better able to identify and embrace your Personal Truths. And when you address your Personal Truths, there is much less compulsion to control. The synergistic interplay between the two can lead to unexpected creative breakthroughs. In the midst of my financial woes,

Paul Eventoff, an artist friend, gave me an hourlong painting lesson, followed by another several months later. As a child, I could not draw, let alone paint—or so I strongly believed. I was thus amazed that in less than a year I was turning out professional-looking still lifes, landscapes, and portraits. I found painting so liberating that I felt grounded by just changing into my painting garb. For me, when I was painting, control was the farthest thing from my mind. I had tapped into an innate gift that I had no inclination I possessed.

Be assured that as you learn to identify your Personal Truths, a healing process begins that allows you to live more in tune with life's natural currents.

CHAPTER SIX

FEAR: CONTROL'S BEST FRIEND

A master of disguise
With tentacles so long,
Flourishing like wild mint
In the tepid soil of our minds.

With us unbeknownst
Its heavy silence so loud, it
Feeds our anxiety, but
Nourishes only our doubts.

Deceit's best lover
So blind-fold brave,
Sharks our dreams,
Tons our creativity.

Yet…truly a coward until unmasked
    Stare its stare,
        Deflect its glare,
           Strip it bare.
Reveal this thing FEAR
For what it truly is,
A wimp hiding in our frail armor
Parading as Fiction's Best Seller.

—*Danny Miller, "Fiction's Best Seller"*

FLASHBACK TO NOVEMBER 2008. Breaking news: investor panic causes Bear Stearns to go belly-up in a few short days. Several weeks later Lehman Brothers goes under. The financial travails reported by the *Wall Street Journal* and CNN grow more alarming by the day. Huge IndyMac Bank is taken over by the Feds. Large European banks are on the verge of insolvency. Pundits use new and confusing financial vocabulary to describe some of the culprits: *Derivatives. Credit default swaps. Mortgage-backed securities.*

In short, we are in a full-blown credit crisis, the likes of which have not been seen since the Great Depression. No one knows when it will end, how bad it will get, or what to do. Everyone blames everyone else, citing a litany of contradictory reasons. Confusion, uncertainty, distrust, and fear abound. Our money may no longer be safe at our own banks. The government is forced to step in to bail out banks and pass emergency legislation that few understand.

Pervasive fear had also entered the life of Reese, a home painting contractor who was finally living the American dream. Three years ago Reese purchased a three-bedroom home with a 5 percent down payment and easy subprime financing. He soon added a swimming pool and outdoor recreation room to the home. He had both an investment account and a retirement account at a large brokerage firm and a savings account at a local bank. His daughter, Kim, just finished her second year of college. Life was good for Reese and his family at the start of 2008.

In the ensuing months, however, Reese took a big hit. The mutual funds and stocks in his brokerage accounts had dropped 35 percent in value. His house decreased 30 percent in value since the beginning of the year. Like many home-owners, he owed more than the house was worth. Moreover, his painting contracts were down 25 percent in October 2008, and November was looking worse. What home-owner wants to continue paying for a house in which he has no equity and when he feels his job may be in jeopardy? Reese cut back on personal and business expenses but was still losing money each month. And how could he tell his daughter that he could not pay next year's college tuition?

Reese was scared—really scared, and depressed. His imagination ran wild. He could hardly sleep. He worried obsessively about all the "what ifs" and "what could happens." His appetite was replaced by intermittent stomach pains and headaches. Reese was literally frozen in his tracks by fear and anxiety. He compensated by becoming very domineering at home and at work. Minor miscues became major grievances. He complained about his wife's cooking, his children making too much noise, and their cats jumping on the furniture. At work, he insisted that everything be done "right now" and threatened to lay people off if they didn't work harder.

Any of this sound familiar? A better question is, What could Reese do about it?

The short answer is that Reese needs to separate facts from fiction so that he can effectively deal with his challenges. Fears are mostly fiction—highly creative fiction that runs rampant unless harnessed by the facts. To overcome his fears, Reese must be courageous. Courage and faith will overtake fear. He thus must face and embrace his fears, which means he must confront and process them. This can be painful (but not nearly as much as you might imagine), but it is the only way he can gain a proper perspective and devise a practical and constructive way to meet his challenges.

This chapter explains how to do this. But first, it is important to examine the connection between fear and control.

FEAR AND CONTROL

Most controllers are fear driven. They are afraid of uncertainty, the unknown, and of what the future holds. Afraid, too, of being harmed if they allow events to take their natural course or people to do their own thing. At their core, controllers fear for their very survival—and their death. To shield themselves from the flames of these demons, they grip life tightly in an attempt to build a fence around their home field.

This effort, however, is fruitless. When you mask your fears, they become even more powerful. They erode your self-confidence, subvert your intuition, and distort reality. As a consequence, normal life concerns appear and feel much worse and more pervasive than they really are or need to be. We feel trapped, and control becomes our escape route.

Moreover, as in Reese's case, fear stokes obsessive worrying and preoccupation with "what if," "what I should do," and "what could happen" rather than accepting and enjoying "what is." These anxieties, in turn, propel people to control even more. They become entrapped in their daily routines and thus are not open to fresh ideas and possible solutions to their problems.

The good news is that when you *lose* fear, you are able to *lose* control and *find* serenity. Being able to identify your fears is the first step in letting them go.

IDENTIFYING YOUR FEARS

For many of us, detecting fear can be quite difficult because fear basks in our ignorance. We tend to attribute the anxiety and discomfort that fear generates to other things. After all, it is much easier and safer to look elsewhere than it is to look within ourselves. Fear is a master of disguise; it easily deceives us. Unfortunately, by the time we unmask its presence, it may have already wreaked considerable havoc. The good news is that exposing fear immediately weakens its hold over us. Once we unmask our fears, we immediately feel less anxiety and begin to see our options more clearly.

I was unable to clearly identify my own fears following the breakup of my first marriage. I was stoic and expressed little emotion. My fears prevented me from getting in touch with my sadness, and my respite was to dive into work, where I could "control" things. It was not until I later identified the fear of being alone that I was able to release much of the heaviness within me.

JANA AND MITCHELL'S KITCHEN WARS

Undetected fear also has a way of wreaking havoc in relationships. My friends Jana and Mitchell are a good example. After dating for several years, they decided to live together. In short order, they began fighting about how the kitchen should be kept. Although Jana was normally a calm person, when it came to maintaining order in the kitchen, she was like a drill sergeant. Mitchell could not understand this sudden mood change that took place almost daily. She was not like that in almost every other aspect of their relationship. And unfortunately, Jana's aggressive behavior triggered strong reactions from him. No one was going to boss Mitchell around! His father had always done so, and as a child Mitchell had no choice but to put up with it—but no more! Jana and Mitchell's relationship was severely rocked by the ongoing kitchen drama.

The couple finally sought counseling. In their sessions it came out that Jana had a great deal of fear about her current situation and about Mitchell's commitment to their relationship. She had returned to college after a five-year absence and was having difficulty adjusting to the competitive university environment. She felt insecure and out of control about school. It lacked order for her. To compensate for this fear, she attempted to assert control and order in her life outside of school, and the kitchen was her chosen arena. Jana was jealous and unfriendly toward Mitchell's young son from a previous marriage because she was insecure about Mitchell's own feelings for her. She was also critical of Mitchell's friends.

In Mitchell's case, he learned he had unprocessed fears from being subservient to a domineering father. He would thus react vehemently when people tried to boss him around. In fact, several times he had even yelled at Jana, "You're not my father!"

Thus Jana's and Mitchell's undetected fears fed upon each other to wreak havoc over what outwardly seemed to be a minor situation. Once their fear-derivative behavior was exposed as such, their "kitchen wars" subsided. Jana was then able to deal with the source of her fear: adjusting to college. For his part, Mitchell was able to respond to her behavior in a more detached manner because he both understood its cause and realized his tendency to overreact.

CONDUCTING A FEAR INQUIRY

One of the best ways to detect this most tricky of emotions is to do a fear inquiry. When you feel unsettled or anxious, take a moment and think about what you might be afraid of. At first you may conclude there is nothing. Push further. The answer might lie in the pit of your stomach or in a tightened chest or throat.

Recall the day's events as specifically as possible. The fear-invoking event will be lurking in there somewhere. More often than not, it will be something you totally blocked—and why not? It was too painful to deal with. The tendency is to move on to more pleasant things. Is it no wonder that by the end of the day, our fears are so deeply buried within us that we cannot identify them? I have had fear-invoking events that I blocked for weeks at a time until they eventually manifested themselves in strong physical symptoms.

In doing your inquiry, be aware of any anger or resentment you may be harboring. Anger is commonly an aggressive response to our fears, and it, too, invokes controlling actions. Still another sure sign of fear is when you procrastinate in addressing important tasks and challenges. During my financial crisis, it was extremely difficult for me to contact new bankers after my loans had been called. Many times I literally couldn't lift the phone to make the necessary calls. It was not until I could pinpoint and process my deep-rooted fear of financial collapse that I could move forward. Likewise, when you find yourself procrastinating over troubling issues, being able to identify your fears is the first step you need to take.

CONFRONTING YOUR FEARS

Once you have a clearer understanding of your fears, the next step is to confront them. Move "closer" to them. Embrace them. Listen to their concerns and apprehensions. Doing this takes true courage, for at this juncture the easiest thing for us is to deflect those fears. However, I can tell you with confidence that if you are able to so "honor" your fears, if only for a short while, their tentacles will begin to loosen their grip and you will experience immediate relief.

Confronting fears requires that you focus on what is truly causing them and then that you stay in the moment with whatever truths are revealed to you. Any method or format you choose to do this in is fine. You will find that the more you confront your fears, the less daunting they become. That is because you strip away the fantasies our minds are so adept at creating. Think of it as wearing a scary mask at Halloween. It is the mask that is frightening, not what is beneath it. Do as I urge in my poem "Fiction's Best Seller," which opens this chapter: "Stare its stare, / Deflect its glare, / Strip it bare."

A WISE SAGE

There is an often-told story of a wise sage and his followers who, during one of their daily walks, come across a pack of fierce dogs. The frightened followers quickly dash in the opposite direction, leaving the sage alone to face the dogs. Instead of running away himself, the sage charges at the dogs. The dogs are so startled that they, too, scamper away. The same dynamic occurs when we embrace our fears because they hate being confronted!

FEEL THE FEAR

As I mentioned earlier, fears have a strong physical presence. Note where they are located—chest, stomach, back, face, or somewhere else—and try to feel their presence. Feel them fully. Don't shy away. As you are focusing on them, take slow, deep breaths through your nose. Draw your breath down to below your navel and feel the physical sensations, then exhale slowly. Be kind to yourself; give yourself permission to feel the fear. You are not a weaker person because of it. Your fears cannot harm you. If you are able to do this, you will soon feel more grounded, and with that your fears will weaken substantially. Remember, fears hate being examined too closely; they know you will soon realize their bark is much worse than their bite.

SHARING YOUR FEARS

Revealing your fears to another person is an excellent way to confront them. Share them with someone you trust. Don't hold back; tell them how frightened you are. The other person often can point out options that you have not seen and reassure you that you will be okay. Your fears will absolutely hate this—trust me. It's bad enough that you have identified them yourself. Exposing them to others is pure blasphemy!

LATE-NIGHT FEARS

Many times fear strikes in the middle of the night. After my bank loans were called, I would wake up about 3:00 a.m. several nights a week from terrifying "financial" nightmares. I could not fall back to sleep because I would think about all the "what ifs" and "what might happens." I laid out strategies while in bed, many of them useful, but I still couldn't sleep. I finally decided to deal with my fears more directly. I got up, had a glass of milk, took out my note pad, and jotted down all the ideas that had been swirling through my mind. Sometimes I actually wrote letters to be sent out the next day. I thus countered my fears by immediately taking steps to address their root causes. As they went from my head to my pad, my anxiety lessened and I was able to fall asleep again.

Becoming Your Own Hero

In my experience, it is harder for men to acknowledge their fears than it is for women because tradition tells us men should be strong and brave. A "real" man isn't afraid. Boys grow up seeing movies and television shows that constantly reinforce this image. As a consequence, many men tend to deny rather than admit their fears and apprehensions. While this image is changing for the better as men become more comfortable in expressing their vulnerability, it is still prevalent. The simple truth of the matter, however, is that the brave have just as many fears as the weak, the difference being that the brave are able to confront their fears. Invariably, when persons are interviewed after performing heroic acts, one of the first statements they typically make is how afraid they had felt.

Thus, in a very real way, you must become your own hero in order to defuse your fears. You must have the courage to confront them. Although this may be daunting at first, any pain or discomfort will be less than imagined and will not last long. The reality is rarely as strong as the imagined harm.

Kate Separates Fact from Fiction

Kate volunteered to be in charge of the annual fundraiser at her child's school. Because of the weak economy, the initial fundraising response was alarmingly weak. Kate became fearful the event would fall far short of expectations and was tormented by the prospect of letting the school down. As the days passed, her anxiety mounted. She didn't know what to do and started to panic.

From past experience, Kate remembered that she needed to confront her fears. She found a quiet place where she could do some deep breathing and try to sense and feel her fears. This was very difficult for her, but Kate knew it was important to work through her discomfort. She continued her deep breathing. After a while she began to feel more grounded and less anxious. At that point, she started separating the "what ifs" from the "what ares." She realized that she needed to regroup and make efficient use of her remaining time.

Kate devised a game plan that focused on the primary sources of fundraising: the school's silent auction and popular internships in the entertainment and sports fields. She made outreach calls to other parent volunteers, enlisting their help in procuring as many internships and items for the silent auction as possible. Then she redirected publicity to these functions.

As Kate implemented these positive steps, her anxiety eased. She even started to have fun with what she was doing—all because she had stripped away the tentacles of her fears so that she could "see" the viable options that were available to her.

MAINTAINING PROPER PERSPECTIVE

Edgar was a Los Angeles flooring contractor whose business had grown steadily over the years. But work started drying up for him in 2007 as a result of the severe economic downturn and decline in home values. Although very concerned and even anxious at times, Edgar didn't panic. He tightened his buckle, cut expenses where possible, and prepared to ride out the market as best he could.

When I asked him how he dealt with his fears, Edgar said, "Things are rough—really rough. I've had to let go of people who've been with me for years, and that was very difficult. But am I real fearful? Am I losing sleep over it? No. And that's because I know that I'm going to be okay. I've been through even rougher times before—both in business and personally—and I'm still here today. I survived then, and I will survive now."

As Edgar's story demonstrates, a highly effective way of defusing fears is to put them in their proper perspective. Think back to times in your life when you had a lot of fears. Were you able to overcome them? Probably more often than not. Did things turn out as badly as you thought they would? Not usually. One more thing is true: you are still around. You have not fallen off some precipice or into a deep pit. The bases of most fears are more illusory than real. If you constantly remind yourself of this, your fears will not undermine you.

Try this simple reassurance exercise (preferably in your own words): "I am afraid and I know the reason. I also know that my fear will pass like it always has in the past, and that I will survive. So, it is okay to feel anxious. That is normal. I will just grin and bear it and let it run its course. It has in the past and it will again. I have faith that I will be okay."

WORST-CASE SCENARIO EXERCISES

An excellent perspective builder is to do a "worst-case scenario" exercise, which was taught to me during my financial crisis by psychologist William Duff. At the time, I had been having nightmares about unsavory people chasing me and finding myself in precarious situations with no way out. Here's how the session went:

Dr. Duff: What would be the worst thing that could happen to you if you are unable to repay your bank loans?

Me: My credit would be shot and the bank would sue me.

Dr. Duff: What would happen then?

Me: The bank would obtain a judgment against me and attach my assets.

Dr. Duff: What then?

Me: I would have to file for bankruptcy.

Dr. Duff: Then what?

Me: I would be broke and out of business.

Dr. Duff: And?

Me (smiling): I would have nothing to do but lie on the beach all day.

What a pleasant thing to do as a worst case. Far different from the foreboding images my imagination had conned me into believing. As I faced my deepest fear and gained proper perspective of my situation, the tension and anxiety immediately left. A month later I persuaded another bank to loan me enough money to pay off the first bank and then some, to boot. I had called fear's bluff, and that's exactly what it was—a bluff.

FICTION'S BEST SELLER

I have discovered many times over that when I reveal and embrace my fears, they run their course and dissipate by themselves, much like a current of water running along the street curb does after it stops raining. My confidence returns, and I can respond intuitively and decisively to address the challenges at hand. Also, I gain a much clearer sense of myself through the experience.

During the banking crisis of the Great Depression, President Franklin Roosevelt movingly and aptly announced to the nation, "The only thing we have to fear is fear itself." Once we are able to recognize this innate truth, we no longer are entrapped by the tentacles of our fears. And the awareness, effort, and considerable courage that you employ to make this happen will help send you on your way to being able to *lose* control and *find* serenity.

CHAPTER SEVEN

ANGER AND RESENTMENT: CONTROL'S NEXT BEST FRIENDS

For every minute you are angry you lose sixty
seconds of happiness.

—*Ralph Waldo Emerson*

Resentment is like drinking poison and waiting for
the other person to die.

—*Carrie Fisher,* Wishful Drinking

MICKEY WAS A HEALTHY ninety-two. Following the death
of his beloved wife, he planned to bequeath each of his four
children an equal share of his savings and the equity in his
home. His oldest daughter, Yolanda, was the only one who
lived nearby and consequently took care of his financial affairs as well as most of his personal needs.

Yolanda's wayward younger sister, Jenna, had recently
moved to a neighboring state with her unemployed hus-

band, Jim, and their young daughter. Mickey, who had always been very concerned about the welfare of Jenna, wanted to help her and Jim buy an old fixer-upper. He asked Yolanda to send a $15,000 check to Jenna from his account. Yolanda, who was struggling with financial pressures of her own and had for years been resentful of her father for not acknowledging all the things she did for him, was perturbed. A month later, Mickey asked her to send her sister another $5,000, which upset Yolanda even more. Over time, Mickey made several more requests, and Yolanda continued to seethe with anger and resentment. Not only had Jenna received more than her fair share, but there appeared to be no end in sight to Mickey's generosity.

In almost every conversation with her other siblings, Yolanda voiced her unbridled fury at what was happening. She was extremely bitter and beside herself and took to drinking more and more. She was truly drinking the "poison" of resentment.

ANGER BREEDS CONTROL

Anger is as much a part of our daily lives as breakfast and dinner. It is a normal consequence of these hectic, impersonal, and dangerous times, when we are forced to deal with computerized voices when calling for repair service or questioning a bill, when other drivers adamantly refuse to let us change lanes, or when high-tech gadgets freeze up. Certainly no one can expect to lead a life totally devoid of anger. In fact, most anger is perfectly normal and at times healthy. For the most part, we forget about the rude driver by the time we reach our destination and chalk up the monotonic computer voices to just a sign of the times.

Of much greater concern, however, is deeply rooted anger and resentment such as Yolanda's, particularly when it is not defused in a timely manner. Such imbedded anger breeds strong control responses. We become closed-minded and rigid. We lash out and intimidate, withdraw and isolate, become obsessed and possessed. And for many, rather than easing the cork out of the champagne bottle, the cork "explodes" in unmitigated rage. When such anger surges without abatement, it ricochets back, more often than not causing harm to someone or something nearby.

My strong propensity was to repress my anger, particularly in business affairs. I felt it important to be civil and even-headed and thus stuffed my anger. As a consequence, I usually did not let people know I was angry or upset. Strangely, sometimes I didn't even know how angry I was! Yet, I took things very personally. I constantly interpreted people's "unfair" or unsavory actions as trying to harm me personally. I never considered that their actions might have been caused by other reasons such as their own insecurities and fears.

Because I did not vent my anger, one of two things invariably occurred. Many times the anger would build up and fester for so long that when it finally did come out, it was with a rage that frightened all those around me. On other occasions it was so deeply repressed that I could not get in touch with it, and I would get depressed and retreat.

IDENTIFYING ANGER

Anger is an important Personal Truth that needs to be processed and defused. As with fear, the first step is to become fully aware of it. Many controllers are not aware of the extent of their anger, so skilled are they at repressing it. They may not feel quite right or feel depressed, yet have little inkling that anger is at the bottom of their discomfort. This may be because many controllers like to think of themselves as reasonable people who should be able to conduct their affairs in a civilized manner. Others feel they are not entitled to express their anger because as children they were not allowed to vent it.

Thus, awareness is the first step in *losing* anger. Since anger is not always outwardly manifested as such, you must look for the clues. Being critical and judgmental of others is often a disguised form of anger, as is withdrawing or closing up. Also, depression can be a direct consequence of unprocessed anger. Getting upset over minor grievances is one of its telltale signs.

An anger inquiry is a good way in which to become more aware of your anger. As in the case of a fear inquiry, ask yourself whether you *feel* angry or resentful about something or somebody. Recount the day's events as specifically as you can. This is not easy; at first you may overlook what you think are minor grievances. However, little "upsets" impact us more than we think.

It is important to clear your mind of all commentary and judgment, and just "sense" and "feel." Remember, too, that anger usually manifests itself physically as well in such forms as muscle tightness, sore back, and headache. Hence, focus on quieting your mind and body—whether through slow breathing, meditating, or another form of mindfulness—and you will soon learn what has angered you.

TECHNIQUES FOR DEFUSING ANGER

Once you become aware of your anger, do not let it fester. Address it. There are a number of safe ways in which this can be done. One is through an imaginary monologue. Imagine that the person with whom you are resentful is standing across the room from you. Tell the person what you think of him or her. Don't be shy. Shout if you wish. No one will think you are a street person talking to yourself. What is nice about this exercise is that it allows you to voice your anger strongly without repercussions. As you vent your anger, it dissipates, and you can then address the "real" issues in a calm and nonconfrontational manner. In Yolanda's case, she could have let her father know that her feelings were hurt because she felt unappreciated, and that she felt her father was not being fair to his other children— especially her—and that his actions were seriously impacting family harmony.

You can also physically release your anger in safe ways. One is with a bataka, a foam-rubber club commonly used by martial artists to safely practice their fighting techniques. (They are available at martial arts equipment stores.) This exercise is quite simple. You get down on your knees, imagine that the person you're angry at is lying on the floor in front of you, and start pounding away with the bataka. And I mean pound! Don't mince words. Start by shouting, "I'm angry!" as you hit the floor with the bataka. Express how mad you are about what that person has done to you. You may feel strange or even embarrassed at first, but soon your emotions will take over and your rage will surge forth. You will be amazed at how quickly your anger and tension disappear.

A similar exercise is to put on boxing gloves and pound a punching bag. In the midst of my lengthy court battle that I have discussed throughout this book, I bought a punching bag and installed it inside my garage. I used it whenever I felt strong anger.

There are many other physical outlets that can reduce anger, such as running, swimming, and playing basketball. Another effective way of exorcizing anger is to vent it on paper. Take a pad and write away. Be as mean as you like. The next time you receive an annoying letter or e-mail from a disgruntled client or friend, don't fire off a response right away. A quick emotional response usually ends up causing more harm than good. (I had a friend who was sued several times for libel because his letters were so nasty.) Instead, write your harsh reply, but don't send it. Once you put your anger on paper, it lessens considerably. I have sometimes left emotional letters on my desk for several days and would then go back and modify them—which is to say, mellow them out—and then mail them.

REMOVE YOUR EXPECTATIONS

Much of our anger is caused by the expectations we set for people and events. When these expectations are not met, we are disappointed and usually upset. This goes for ourselves as well. When we expect too much of ourselves, we get upset at you-know-who when we fail to meet them. The solution to all this is very simple: remove or at least lower your expectations. You'll have fewer disappointments.

Healing the Heart
with Forgiveness

Although quite effective, the above exercises are more temporal in nature. Removing deeply rooted anger and resentment from betrayal, rejection, abuse, abandonment, and the like requires much more. Such anger and resentment are based mostly on past transgressions—some a lifetime in duration—and dealing with them only through management techniques like the ones above will not always reduce them effectively.

You need to heal your "heart wounds," and forgiveness is the key because it releases the bitter thought waves and preoccupation with the past. I know this can be extremely difficult, even unbearable. After all, why should you forgive the very people who harmed you? However, ask yourself: What do I gain by holding on, and what might I lose by letting go? The answer to both these questions is more often than not a resounding NOTHING.

Finding Forgiveness

Finding the means to forgive is very personal and may best be done with the guidance and support of a trained therapist. I offer a few ways below that have worked well for myself and others.

Prayer and Meditation

The healing power of prayer can be very effective. Consider praying for the strength and courage to let go of your anger, to forgive and forget. Reflect and meditate on whether you have judged too harshly or jumped to unfounded conclusions about other people's actions.

ACKNOWLEDGING YOUR OWN ROLE

You should always consider whether you had some role in the anger-provoking occurrence. It takes courage and self-honesty to admit you may be at fault as well—at least partially. For example, you may have been smug or discourteous in your interactions with someone, and that provoked the person. You may have pressured someone too much to do what you wanted, thereby causing resentment.

A good example of how I wasn't as innocent as I thought occurred during spring soccer season for our daughter Lana, then age twelve. My wife, Sigute, would drive us to the games, which were held on a field adjacent to the Rose Bowl in Pasadena, California. Even though this was a weekly trip for us, she would often forget which freeway exit to use. It would take us ten minutes to get back on track. She became very frustrated every time this happened and would start blaming me. I of course was resentful. Why was it my fault? I wasn't the one driving. I wasn't the one who kept making the same mistake.

The day after the last of these misdirectional mishaps (after the "embers" had cooled), she and I were able to talk about it calmly. When I asked her how I could be at fault for these repeated occurrences—feeling there was absolutely no way—she told me that the air was "thick" with my anxiety that she would again take the wrong exit, so she lost her concentration and did exactly what I feared. I had to admit that was absolutely true because I was indeed always worried and thinking just that.

So I did have a role in what happened, even though I initially could not see it. Similar experiences convinced me that no matter how innocent or right I thought I was about the person or event that triggered my anger, I was in some way responsible. I may not be able to see it right away, but after a while—sometimes even several days—I am able to recognize the role I played.

FINDING THE GOOD

Before I learned how to forgive, I experienced the severe harms of unrelenting resentment. This happened during my all-consuming battle with my former business partner, whom I felt had betrayed me in my weakest moment. The specific facts are not important, and I doubt that I could fairly recount them today, so enraged was I at the time. However, my rage and resentment were very real. I literally felt like a lamb being led to slaughter, and that propelled me to fight and resist and to control at all costs, including my health.

This obsessive, costly, and foolhardy battle went on for five years and brought me to the brink of bankruptcy. It also severely impacted my relationship with my young son and contributed to the breakdown of my first marriage. Yet, even ending up in the hospital and going through six major surgeries didn't cause me to relent. A part of me knew I badly needed to get out of this cesspool, and yet I couldn't find a way. My rage was still too powerful.

Then one day a close, wise friend asked whether I could ever forgive my adversary. I remember my response so clearly: "Are you kidding! Look what he's done to me! Why should I forgive him?"

"Because it would be better for you," my friend calmly responded. "It is the only way you'll ever be able to extricate yourself from the accelerating pressures and burdens you're enduring and move on with your life."

"That may be so," I said, "but to forgive him would be admitting defeat. It would be letting him get away with what he did to me, and all my efforts in seeking vindication would be out the window. I don't think I could live with that. And besides, I wouldn't know how to forgive him even if I wanted to."

My friend asked how I thought my partner viewed me. Never having considered that, I took a few minutes to think, and then with a sheepish smile answered: "I'm sure he must consider me a young upstart who has been ungrateful for all the things he's done for me, such as helping me establish a good banking relationship with his bank and introducing me to his business associates. I'm also sure that he must have tremendous anger toward me for tying up his valuable property during the litigation. He's always used to having total control over everything and everyone, and I have prevented that. And I am sure he is fuming at the idea that the value of my interest in the property has increased over 800 percent during the case through his efforts in managing it."

"How does all that make you feel?" my friend asked.

"Pretty good," I mused. "I can now see that he must feel betrayed as well. That allows me to at least understand why he's been such an SOB. I'm sure he feels his actions have been justified, and maybe some of them were; I don't know. I don't feel nearly as resentful right now, but still, the idea of forgiving him is not easy."

When I saw my friend again several weeks later, he asked me how things were going with my big battle. I told him that at a meeting with our attorneys I had talked to my former partner for the first time in over three years.

Although it felt strange, I liked not being as angry as I had been for so long, but I still was afraid to let him know I wanted to settle the suit.

My friend questioned why, and I replied, "I don't know how to begin without showing weakness. My adversary is an extremely wealthy and powerful person. You have to be very firm with him or he'll walk all over you. He will likely view any conciliatory gesture on my part as a sign of weakness. But I know deep down that it's best for me and my family to get out of this terrible mess."

My friend then asked if I could think of any ways that my adversary had helped me, even unwittingly. At first I was puzzled by the question. However, after reflecting for a moment, I offered, "Well, one thing I know, I learned an awful lot from him during the years we worked together. He's a very astute businessman. In fact, I have been able to apply what I learned from him in my own business dealings with great success. And some of the people he introduced me to have turned out to be good clients."

I paused for a moment, then continued. "But you know something—I just thought of this—he has played a major role in helping me prove to myself that I can take care of myself under severe pressure and adverse circumstances. I always had doubts about that. What better proof do I need than to know that I've given this very powerful person the fight of his life? I've managed to draw upon my inner resources and talents to resist him every step of the way. I never knew I could be so resourceful. He's tried to squeeze me whenever he could, and I'm still here and haven't caved in."

"It seems," my friend observed, "that this man has provided you with many blessings—blessings that perhaps you could not have received in any other way, strange as that may seem."

"You know, I think you're right," I responded. "Boy, life is really strange sometimes. At this moment I have absolutely no anger toward him. I actually feel sorry for him. I wish him no ill will."

Several months later I was able to settle the lawsuit without being ramrodded as I had feared I would. It turned out that my former partner was also anxious to settle. At a celebration dinner party at my favorite restaurant, I stood and gave a heartfelt toast to the man (in absentia) for everything he had done for me and wished him well.

I thus learned that forgiveness is essential for eradicating deeply rooted anger and resentment. It is the best and perhaps the only real means of healing your heart wounds and putting the past behind you. It enables you to focus on what is truly important and meaningful in your life.

When you *lose* anger, you are able to *lose* control and *find* some peace. I believe the results speak for themselves.

CHAPTER EIGHT

AVOIDING AVOIDANCE

Engulfed with anger,
We retreat.
Ensnared by fear,
We hide.

Webbed by doubts,
We avoid.
Immersed in pities,
We remain
In exile—
With no default mode.

To return,
Joust the fears,
Lose the anger,
Embrace the truth, and
Face the danger.

—*Danny Miller, "Default Mode"*

I LEARNED THE SEVERE consequences of avoidance when I delayed taking action to confront a group of juveniles who were skateboarding up the walls and on the railings of a Nevada office building I owned. When my manager first reported the problem to me, I listened but did nothing. I silently hoped it would go away by itself and promptly found other things at work to occupy my time.

A week later, graffiti appeared on the walls of the building. Several tenants threatened to leave because of it. I was very upset but still did nothing, preferring to see the vandalism as an isolated event. I did feel unsettled about it, though, and believe it or not, I had little inkling why. Denial was a strong suit of mine at the time!

Several days later, one of our tenants was burglarized. Finally, I acted. We gated the exposed rear entrance to the building. I thought that would do the job. But several days after that, the juveniles broke the lock and continued to loiter after hours. I then extended the working hours of the manager of the building so that he would be at the property when the kids were most likely to cause trouble. I also placed large planters in the courtyard to prevent skateboarding up the walls. Lo and behold, this worked. I finally confronted the problem and avoided further damage and anguish.

As time went on, I became better at addressing problems and unpleasant tasks earlier. Yet, looking back, I know I could have saved myself and my tenants a lot of anguish had I dealt with events as they arose. We may try to "bury" things, but that doesn't mean they go away. They are still present, albeit in the far reaches of our minds, where they are nourished and magnified by our fears.

When we use avoidance, we direct and manipulate our thoughts and actions away from important life challenges and issues. In doing so, we control others and events and hurt ourselves as well as those around us.

SUSAN THE PROCRASTINATOR

A good example of how the avoidance dynamic works is illustrated by Susan, who failed to RSVP to an important family event. Susan is one of those people who waits until the last minute to do something, particularly if she doesn't want to do it. Her constant dilemma is that she doesn't want to disappoint others by putting her needs first, but at the same time doesn't believe that her needs are entitled to any priority. Consequently, she frequently delays taking any action at all until the very last minute, resulting in hurt feelings and inconveniencing others.

Finally, Susan outdid herself. She had been invited to a bridal shower for her husband's cousin's daughter, whom she barely knew. This cousin was very close with Susan's mother-in-law, Bernice. The shower was in another city, about an hour and a half's drive away. Susan didn't want to take a day out of her busy schedule to attend the shower, but she put off responding to the invitation because she didn't want to disappoint Bernice. The bride-to-be contacted Bernice two days before the shower, inquiring as to whether Susan was going to attend. Bernice, who didn't know that Susan had failed to RSVP, was put on the spot and embarrassed by her daughter-in-law's poor etiquette. She promptly called Susan to voice her displeasure over what had transpired. Susan, ashamed, called and left a message that she was not attending the event.

PROCRASTINATION AND OVERCOMING IT

The two most prevalent types of avoidance are procrastination and withdrawal.

Procrastination results in lost opportunities. When you delay in addressing obstacles, opportunities to resolve them pass by. Moreover, unattended problems easily mushroom into larger and often unmanageable ones; if you finally do address them, more time and energy are required to resolve them.

Awareness is thus a prerequisite to taking action. Sometimes we are not consciously aware we have problems that need addressing. We are in denial. But on some level, we know the problems are there. Anxiety and discomfort, including physical symptoms, can serve as a guide. When you are feeling low or depressed, consider whether you are avoiding something important.

Procrastination is primarily fear based. We have seen how fear can freeze you in your tracks. You become so absorbed with the "what ifs" and "what could happens" that you are afraid to take any action at all. The following worst-case scenario exercise is an excellent tool in this regard. If you are hesitant to act, project the worst things that could happen through a series of "what if" inquiries so that you can get everything out on the table. As you do, try to separate fact from fiction. Then map out an action plan should your worst fears materialize (in most cases they will not, because they were either illusory or insignificant). By having a plan, the potential problems will feel less daunting and your fears will diminish, allowing you to effectively meet your challenges head-on.

If you are uncertain where to begin, test the waters. Make a to-do list and do the first thing on it. It may be rereading the divisive demand letter you received from your competitor's attorney or responding to your bank's request for additional financial information on an investment that is not doing well. Perhaps it is returning the call of an irate customer, meeting with your boss to express your misgivings about your job or issues you have with a co-worker, or starting a daily workout routine to improve your health. Whatever the first step, taking it will make you feel much better. The problem will lose much of its fright—and might.

Do not let yourself be deterred if you do not at first have an inkling of the ultimate solution to the problem. Just lose some control—stop projecting and fretting—and allow events to unfold by themselves. At some point, a probable solution may emerge, and you can then act on it. If that prospect fizzles out, wait for another path to open up for you. Eventually you should find a path that leads to a workable resolution. At the very least, even if you are unsuccessful in resolving your obstacles, you will eliminate the ongoing anxiety caused by procrastination.

WITHDRAWAL: MISSING OUT

Withdrawal removes you from life's "possibilities." At times we all have had the urge to retreat and "hole up" and just escape from the world. This is understandable given the burdens and pressures of the world we live in. It is often easier to withdraw into our private world of painful thoughts and self-pity than it is to confront vital issues head-on. And for controllers, withdrawal comes faster, deeper, and more often than it does for most people. This should come as no surprise. When you are preoccupied with controlling people and things, it is easy to lose sense of who you are and how you truly feel. Thus, you become alienated from the world around you.

RETURNING FROM EXILE

The danger, however, is that withdrawal can become a self-perpetuating process. The longer your departure, the more difficult your return, and by the time you finally resurface, considerable harm may already have been done. At home, your mates and family may feel rejected and helpless, even abandoned. The same is true with close friends. When you withdraw at work, it becomes difficult to focus on important job assignments, as well as to interact with co-workers and customers. In sports, your performance becomes lackluster. In the arts, your creativity is submerged. And with intimate relations, your sex drive disappears.

In short, when you withdraw, you miss out on what life has to offer.

Because of its negative momentum, withdrawal needs to be nipped in the bud. The key is to learn what makes you withdraw and then counter it in a timely manner. For example, review the history of your deepest withdrawals and determine the things that caused your exit. For many, unprocessed fear and resentment are catalysts. It may be financial fears or fear of deteriorating personal relationships. It may be harboring resentment from having to "do battle" at work all the time or from being let down by others. Grief and sadness, particularly from the loss of a loved one or a close relationship, are also prevalent causes of withdrawal.

To return from your personal "exile," these core feelings and emotions need to be processed; otherwise they will fester, propelling you deeper into your inner sanctum.

TRUTH CENTERING

"Truth centering" is a good way to process these Personal Truths. As you already know, truth centering can take many forms, including prayer, meditation, and exercise. You may wish to sit or lie down in a quiet place and do some deep breathing while trying to pay attention to your feelings. Be sure to get in touch with any physical symptoms and discomfort, such as tightness in your stomach, back, or head. As you do, take care not to be self-critical or judgmental. Be kind to yourself. You are entitled to feel the things you do, even self-pity. Your grief needs to be processed. At some point, you will feel more grounded, allowing you to begin to address the very problems that caused you to retreat.

Another way of returning from your self-imposed exile is by revealing your unwanted feelings to someone else. Choose to work with a "return guide," usually your mate or a trusted friend. You may feel uncomfortable at first, but keep in mind that it is far easier than the pain of isolation. Start by expressing to your return guide what you feel, whether it is loneliness, sadness, anger, fear, or the like. This very acknowledgment helps considerably because you are *including* someone in your private world. Your guide can then help you probe deeper as to what is troubling you and how you may overcome your challenges. This process gives you permission to open up, and as you get more in touch with your feelings, the negative energy stored within you is released. Before long, you will begin to return from exile.

Be Your Own Guardian

Another way to return from exile is to act as your own guardian. This method was taught to me by family therapist Barbara LaSalle. Here is how it works. If you are at home, move to the opposite side of the room. Sit down and look back at your "other" self. Observe that fragile little person—your inner child—and sense how he or she feels. Is he looking disconsolately down at the floor? Is she slouched on the sofa? Does he look as if he is carrying the weight of the world on his shoulders?

Next, the other, more detached "you" should reach out to help this vulnerable person. Comfort and reassure him. Let her know that everything will be okay, that you understand her fears and anxieties, that her burdens will not last, that she will survive. You can do this because you are not caught up in your little person's fears and anxiety. Your guardian self is more confident, objective, and aware; she knows she can take care of both "yous."

These exercises work well because when you withdraw, you unwittingly deprive yourself of what you need most: reassurance. If no one is available to give it to you, you must learn how to give it to yourself.

PART III

LOSING CONTROL
IN ALL THE RIGHT PLACES

CHAPTER NINE

LOSING PARENTAL CONTROL: *REDUCING* THE STRUGGLE

Your children are not your children...
they come through you but not from you.
And though they are with you yet
they belong not to you...
You may give them your love but not your thoughts,
For they have their own thoughts...
Seek not to make them like you.

—*Kahlil Gibran,* The Prophet

VICTORIA NEVER PLAYED SOCCER herself, but she became an avid fan of the sport in a short amount of time. Soccer brought out Victoria's competitive spirit. When her twelve-year-old son, Tim, made the all-star AYSO team, Victoria was only too happy to take him to the two weekday practices and the weekend games. Tim loved playing, and he worked hard to improve his game. He was making steady progress, but this was not fast enough for Victoria. In her mind, Tim was not trying hard enough. She believed that he needed to be more aggressive to reach the "next level." Nothing irked her more than to see another player beat her son to the ball.

And so Victoria, ever the controller, constantly pushed Tim to be more aggressive on the field. Her shouts could be heard above everyone else's. Tim complained to his mom that she was distracting him during the game. But this didn't deter her. During one important tournament game, Victoria loudly criticized Tim in front of the other parents for backing off some bigger opponents. Tim was so embarrassed that he walked off the field crying, right in the middle of the game. He told Victoria he didn't want to play anymore.

Unfortunately, such stories are all too common in childhood sports. To see what's really at stake, just go to a league game in almost any sport and witness who suffers most from a loss and who takes longer to get over it! Here's a clue: it is not the child.

Excessive parental control extends well beyond the playing field. It pervades the classroom, artistic performance, religious observance, childhood friendships, and social activities, all with equally troubling consequences.

Parental Control: Crossing the Line

Parental control comes in a variety of forms, many appropriate and some not: assertive (commands, discipline), gentle (persuading and cajoling), vocal (shouting and yelling), passive (withdrawal and abandonment), emotional (shaming), and physical (hitting and spanking).

There is no question that control is an integral part of parenting. I like to refer to appropriate forms of parental control as parental authority or parental guidance. These forms of control are essential not only for a child's health and safety but also for fostering a child's morals, family values, and ethics; social manners and etiquette; and learning. Indeed, parental authority is fundamental to a healthy parent-child relationship, and parents would be irresponsible not to exercise it.

The key is knowing when parental control crosses the line and becomes harmful. Domineering parental control in most cases is unhealthy and even harmful to children. It is also counterproductive. The extreme case, of course, is when a parent emotionally or physically demeans or abuses the child, but much less intense forms can also impact the child's well-being. Admittedly, the distinction between appropriate parental authority and parental domination is not always clear. Generally speaking, domineering control is usually triggered by a parent's own motives, ego, fears, and anxieties. And while there are occasions when strong control measures may be necessary and justified, care should always be taken not to harm a child's natural spirit.

I describe below some factors that will assist in determining whether parental control is excessive.

Am I Obstructing My Child's Personal Growth and Life Path?

Parental control becomes harmful when a child's personal growth and life path is obstructed by the parent. I firmly believe that every child is unique, with his or her own (and, I believe, God-given) nature, talents, and life journey, and a parent's role is to foster that. I thus try to remember that it is "thine journey, not mine." When we try too hard to influence or change our children's intrinsic nature and life path, we risk not only diminishing our children but also driving them away—emotionally and physically. This is not to say that a parent should not encourage and share in the joy of a child's growth and development and achievements. Simply put, parental involvement should be supportive and loving, rather than motivated by a parent's unfulfilled dreams, social standing, and the like.

One parent explained it to me this way: "I realized that my anxiety about Amber was mine, not hers, and that I really can't influence her life. I tried, and it doesn't work that way. It's a giant waste of time. It was only when I learned to let go that good things happened with her.

"Amber has her own life journey, and I don't want to take that away from her. She will do what she does on her own time. She was late in learning to crawl and I was really concerned about that, so I tried all kinds of things to teach her to crawl, without success. Then I just stopped doing that, and she started crawling two weeks later. The same thing with her piano lessons. I wanted her to learn classical music, and she kept resisting. So I stopped giving her lessons. A few years later after a voice lesson she started playing a few chords on the piano, and before I knew it she was avidly learning how to play the piano to accompany her singing. Same thing happened with school. Amber was always a typical B student, and I fretted that she wasn't going to get into college. Then in the eighth grade, on her own, she started studying more and getting straight As.

"I am now very clear that my role is to love and care for her, support her, keep her as safe as I can, and let go of just about everything else. And what joy Amber gives me!"

What Is My Motive?

It is important to consider the motive behind parental control actions. For example, is it to satisfy the ego or needs of the parent—including avoiding possible embarrassment—or to serve the higher need of the child? Parental pressure for children to do better or perform better is often based on parents' egos rather than on enhancing a child's self-esteem. Sports, competitions, and performance are popular arenas for control-driven parental egos. Many parents push their children to excel in music, sports, or academics, for example, to where the child feels overburdened and overstressed. The parent becomes the taskmaster who insists on performance well beyond the child's abilities. It seems that nothing the child achieves or does is good enough. Such domination most often adversely impacts performance; the child may clam up or even panic because he or she is not calm and relaxed enough to perform to his or her ability. Taken to the extreme, such domination can trigger resentment and rebellion.

Is My Way the Right Way?

As parents, we often believe that what has worked for us in our own lives—or the ways we were taught by our parents—is equally good for our children. This is not necessarily true. Take my friend Sandra, whose parents were very "old school" regarding piano lessons. They hired a demanding, humorless instructor who relentlessly hammered Sandra with "proper" technique. Sandra became quite proficient but never truly enjoyed playing piano. Yet, Sandra, without giving it a second thought, constantly hovered over her own daughter, Lisa, when she was learning to play piano. Eventual result: Lisa stopped playing piano altogether.

Genetics aside, our children are not nearly as much like us as we think. Yes, they look and act like us in varying ways, but they are very different from us. This point was powerfully driven home to me when I pressured my daughter Lana (then ten years old) to prepare for an important test. I wanted her to do it the way I had done it in school (making study notes, outlining the material, etc.), not by listening to loud rock music. She promptly responded: "Daddy, I'm different than you. I can't do it that way. Listening to music helps me study better."

I was immediately taken aback by the simple truth of what she said. Lana really is different than me, and vastly so. She studies for tests and does her homework differently than I did. She budgets her time differently than I did. She keeps her room and desk much differently than I did. She also has many different interests and talents than I had. After all, who am I to say that my way is the best way—for her? My way is just a way, nothing more. It worked for me, but that doesn't mean it works for my child.

Over time I came to learn that I serve my children best when I act as a loving mentor and supporter and, when necessary, as their protector. I accomplish this best when I am willing to *lose* some control and allow them to make their own choices and bear the results and consequences of those choices. Moreover, I try to offer advice only when they seek my counsel, and interestingly, they seek it much more when I don't volunteer it.

AM I ENABLING MY CHILD?

Parental enabling is another form of harmful control because it deprives children of learning the important lesson of accepting responsibility for their actions or lack thereof.

Enabling is prominently played out in school, where many parents actually do much, sometimes all, of their children's homework assignments and class projects. The parents' intentions may be good, but such control deprives the child of the opportunity to learn and be independent. Moreover, there is less incentive for the child to work hard because the child knows the parent is there to correct his or her mistakes. Finally, it denies teachers the opportunity to discover students' shortcomings and help to improve them.

Clearly, it is often difficult to distinguish between being a "loving" parent and an "enabling" one. To assist in that regard, ask yourself the following questions:

* Am I depriving my child of learning from her mistakes or of gaining other important learning experiences?

* Will any real harm come to my child if I don't help this time?

* Is my child's health and safety involved?

* Will it make my child more dependent on me?

* Could I handle it if my child "fails" this time?

Is My Control Fear Based?

We have already seen how fear is a prime control generator in most life arenas, and no less so when striving to be a responsible parent. We are afraid that harm will come to our children if we loosen the reins or let them fend for themselves. We don't trust they will make the right choices. We do not want our children to make the same mistakes as we did. We are thus prone to do more when less is better.

Much of the time, we have difficulty separating the facts from the nightmares that our emotions script for our children. It is always helpful to consider how important the issues really are. What is truly at stake? Is it a crisis or just a minor disturbance? Consider whether you have to do anything right away and what might happen if you don't intervene. Many problems concerning our children are not crises and resolve themselves with the simple passage of time—as long as we don't interfere.

HILLARY FEARS FOR MAYA

Maya is a typical sixth grader who puts off studying for tests until the last minute, including final exams. This doesn't sit well with her mother, Hillary. Hillary insists that Maya start studying at least three days before an exam. Maya resists, Hillary insists. Maya talks back, Hillary punishes. Maya refuses to study, Hillary punishes more. Maya throws a tantrum, Hillary is beside herself.

Now, let's examine Hillary's worst fears if she allowed Maya to prepare for a test her own way. One fear would be that Maya will get a poor grade. What might be worse? That Maya will fail the test altogether. What still could be worse—I mean really bad? Maya might not be able to get into a good college.

Let's consider what Hillary can do to get some perspective and deal with her worst fears. She can start by trying to separate fact from fiction (and emotions). Maya may very well do poorly on her exams and even fail some. However, does it follow that she will fail the subject? Perhaps, but not likely. Will it impact her chances of getting into a good college? Highly unlikely—she is only in the sixth grade. However, even if this very "worst case" were to occur, does it mean that Maya will be unhappy and not do well in life?

Unlikely. The cases are legion about highly successful people who fared poorly in school.

Consider a scenario that is just as likely to occur: If Maya does poorly on her tests, her teacher will likely talk to her to find out why and maybe even offer to help. Maya may also be embarrassed by her classmates knowing how poorly she did, and this may motivate her to improve her study habits, even possibly following her mother's advice.

There is still another scenario to consider—maybe the most likely, in fact: Maya actually may do well on her tests because cramming serves a certain purpose for her. She simply may concentrate better under pressure.

BUILDING A FAMILY DEMOCRACY

If you think about it, from a child's perspective the parent always has the upper hand. What a parent says usually goes. The child feels he must constantly give in and has little or no say in decisions that impact his life. This vast control inequality promotes resistance and discord. Is it any wonder that most children can't wait until they grow up and are able to make their own decisions and choices? Consequently, relinquishing some control in parenting fosters a healthier and happier parent-child relationship. Notice that I say "some" control. You don't need to give up final say or relegate your parental responsibilities. The ultimate goal is to encourage a participatory family democracy based on open communication, honesty, trust, and a safe environment in which to express contrarian views. Giving up some parental control is essential for accomplishing this. Promoting a participatory family democracy early on reduces insolence and rebellion later for the simple reason that there is much less to rebel against.

Negotiating between parent and child provides more harmonious "contractual" control. Thus, for example, when a child resists completing her homework (or a similar task), instead of adamantly insisting that she continue—particularly if backed with threats or severe consequences—which invites confrontation, compromise a bit and allow the child to take a break or do something fun, with the mutual agreement that the task be completed later within a certain time frame, lest there be pre-established consequences. Be very clear and specific about the terms of the agreement. Repeat it several times.

Similarly, allowing a child some say in setting bedtime can be fruitful. Let's say that you would like 9:30 to be "lights out" for your fifth grader. Rather than issuing the order, you might consider saying to her: "Okay, you can go to bed at either 9:00, 9:20, or 9:30—your choice." She will naturally select 9:30 but will likely do so willingly because she participated in the decision. Giving up some control in this manner allows the child to participate in the decision-making process, for which the child will usually be willing to accept greater responsibility.

Another effective way to give up parental control is to hear the child out. Listening to his or her views and concerns levels the playing field and empowers the child, even if the parental decision remains essentially the same. Just as important, it can also draw out information from which you as a parent can make more informed decisions. A child's troublesome behavior might be influenced by the fact that she is upset over not being invited to a birthday party or other social event, or she might be feeling anxiety about taking an important test. Not making a sports team or doing poorly on an exam can have similar effects.

Attentive listening can also have a powerful healing effect because it allows the child to express his or her concerns instead of keeping them sealed within. In this regard, it is important to listen without trying to solve the child's "problems" or criticize his or her behavior. Most often, children want to express their concerns, not receive advice.

Knowing Where Your Power Lies

At times we need to accept that we are powerless over certain matters concerning our children, and that trying to control their resolution is doomed from the start. I vividly remember when my daughter Lana was misbehaving just prior to her sixth birthday party. Twenty children had been invited and were due to arrive at our home in three hours. Lana was getting under my skin so much that I shouted, "You keep that up and I'm cancelling your birthday party!"

Even at that young age, she knew full well that I couldn't follow through with my control threat. Hence, she was quickly in my face shouting, "No, you're not, Daddy, you know you can't!" Clearly, I had lost control instead of *losing* control. I have since learned two important things about setting consequences. The first is that I must have the power to enforce them. The second is that they should be stated in a calm, anger-free manner—and this sometimes means waiting a day until I have processed my anger.

Knowing where your power lies is very important in dealing with serious issues affecting your child. Take, for example, parents who have discovered that their teenager is using drugs. I have heard many parents share that their first reaction was to angrily confront their child, insist that he or she stop, and set strict consequences for continued use.

Almost all these parents reported that this method worked only for a while at best. The reality was that their children found ways to use drugs again when they wanted to, short of the parents spending every moment of their day (and night) tracking them.

The point here is that there are limits on what parents can do in such complex situations, and when they act forcefully out of fear and anger, they risk exacerbating the situation. It is more useful to focus on what you as a parent effectively have the power to do. If you are in a precarious situation, you have the power to do nothing right away. That's right: you have the power to *lose* control. Instead, reflect, meditate, pray, and/or seek counsel until you are more clear about how to address the problem. You also have the power to process your anger, fear, and other strong emotions evoked by your child's actions. You can later speak to your child in a calmer manner, coming from a perspective of love and concern for his or her health and safety, conveying that you are genuinely concerned about his or her well-being. You can discuss the real-life consequences of continued drug use, including brain damage or death, poor grades, failure to get into college, and so forth.

Further, by so enhancing the lines of communication, you may learn the underlying reasons for the destructive behavior, such as peer pressure, a need to be liked, or other reasons that make it difficult for your child to say no. You can then attempt to address those issues in a constructive, caring manner and establish a mutual game plan for reducing the risks. One such method offered by some parenting professionals is to establish a "code word." If your child is in a high-risk situation, he or she phones you and says the code word. No questions are asked and you immediately go remove him or her from the high-risk encounter.

None of this, it should be noted, precludes setting strict consequences if your child continues to indulge. However, the consequences can be discussed with your child and jointly agreed upon in advance, so that if the occasion later arises, you can remain calm.

SOME FINAL THOUGHTS

Today many parents are frustrated and distressed because they feel they have lost control of their children. Things have gotten too out of hand for many—and for some, alarmingly so. The natural inclination for such parents is to become more controlling in their efforts to contain the damage. Hence, they typically become more demanding, punishing, resistant, and closed-minded in their interactions with their children, unwittingly exacerbating the problem.

To these parents, I would offer that the chance for success in *regaining* control of your children lies instead in *losing* forceful parental control over them by learning to accept "what is" within the context of your specific situation, and working within that essential parameter. This means that you must accept—for now, at least—that you are powerless over (and cannot change) certain factors within your child's life and within your relationship with your child, and instead devote your time and energy to improving those things over which you do have some control, or which you can change. The latter includes your attitudes, expectations, reactions, and engagements with respect to your children, as well as confronting and defusing your own fears, anxiety, and anger.

CHAPTER TEN

LOSING LOVE CONTROL: *FINDING* ROMANCE AND INTIMACY

"The beginning of love is to let those we love be perfectly themselves, and not to twist them to fit our own image. Otherwise we love only the reflection of ourselves we find in them."

—*Thomas Merton: "No Man Is an Island" (1955)*

LOVE AND ROMANCE ARE fertile grounds for controlling actions. The two stories that follow are prime examples.

Don had met Karin on the rebound. Heartbroken after losing his childhood sweetheart to another man, he had gone abroad for two years on a church mission. That's how he met Karin. The two twentysomethings dated for a year. Don was convinced that they were meant for each other, and he bought her an engagement ring. Karin accepted the ring somewhat reluctantly. She was not sure it was wise to get married at such a young age. Don pressed Karin to set a wedding date, but she wanted to proceed slowly. Don simply didn't understand; he was absolutely sure that they were perfect for each other. He thus kept trying to convince Karin of the merits of his view. He even solicited her father, who liked Don, to talk to her about it.

Finally, the pressure became so great for Karin that she ended the engagement. Don was stunned. How could this happen to him again? A few weeks later, he had what he called a love epiphany that ended his grieving. He realized that he could not control how or what a loved one felt no matter how convinced he was otherwise. That was simply beyond his power. Don kept this valuable lesson in mind from then on. Eventually he met and married a lovely woman who shared his optimism about their union. The two have enjoyed a solid marriage for over twenty years and have two wonderful children.

The second story involves Kathy. In her twenties, Kathy was a passionate romantic who freely gave of herself whenever she was in love. But twice she had endured tremendous heartbreak. Leery of being hurt again, she dedicated herself to her career in marketing, where she found great success. She liked the structure and control that her work brought. She could call the shots. She was the one who "let go" of others.

Yet, Kathy missed having a man in her life. Over the years she had relationships, but they were always on her terms. She could not bear the thought of more painful breakups. She thus chose men who allowed her to dictate when and how often they would see each other, where they would go, and what they would do. These men were the opposite of her early loves, who were strong and independent. They were nice but weak and dependent on her.

Kathy could never give fully to these relationships, and her passions remained unfulfilled. Ultimately, she would tire of these men and the relationships would break up.

LOVE CONTROL: THE BLANKET OF FEAR

Love control runs the gamut from unsolicited advice and opinions, to criticism and judgment, to unreasonable demands and agendas. When we behave in this way with our partners, our actions invariably diminish the love glow and breed resentment. People don't like being told what to do, how to be, or how to act in matters of the heart.

Control forces the action rather than allowing the give-and-take of a relationship to unfold in its own time. As in most control-driven environments, fear is the primary catalyst of love control: fear of not finding or keeping someone, of not being attractive or good enough, and of being alone. The "real" person is covered by this blanket of fear and not seen for whom he or she is.

SEARCHING FOR THE "RIGHT" PERSON

The song "Lookin' for Love (in All the Wrong Places)," sung by Johnny Lee, encapsulates a prevalent control mechanism for many people seeking love and romance: SEARCHING. People constantly search for love and romance (in all places!) and go to great extremes trying to find it. They have high expectations and pursue them rigorously, be it through clubs, mixers, blind dates, dating services, and on the Internet. Most are repeatedly disappointed because love control forces the dancers to be out of step with the music. The dance of romance loses its rhythm.

It is more than just coincidence that those who are not preoccupied with finding the "right" person frequently find the right person. They find because they are not looking. They find because they have fewer expectations. They find because their "vision" is not obscured by preconceived notions and inflexible agendas. They find because *losing* control in matters of the heart allows "love" currents to flow naturally and openly, and one's inner beauty to shine through.

I know this from personal experience. Over fifteen years ago, I met a very nice—but not my "type"—woman at a charity event. She had recently broken up with her boyfriend. Not only had she decided to forgo dating, she mused about entering a convent in Italy (talk about giving up control!). At the time, I was a single parent raising my young daughter Lora (then age three), and I, too, was not seeking a serious relationship. In fact, I wasn't even going to ask for her telephone number until a good friend graced me with these words of wisdom, for which I shall forever be grateful: "Danny, take her number. You can always decide later if you want to call her!"

Neither of us had any expectations, which left little at stake. From there things just flowed—so smoothly and beautifully, in fact, that we were married two years later. We both had found our "hidden treasure" where least expected.

LOVE ENABLERS

Love enablers are controllers who devote themselves to taking care of and doing things for their loved ones, usually at the expense of not taking care of their own needs. Good intentions aside, their actions are controlling because they deprive their loved ones of the satisfaction of taking care of themselves and the dignity and growth associated with it. Love enablers also set themselves up for disappointment when they fail to be "appreciated." This easily can become a double-edged sword with both parties being harmed: the enabler is resentful for the lack of gratitude and having ignored his own needs, and the loved one feels intruded upon. In short, when you give too much in love, you take away from your loved one—and from yourself.

The enabling control dynamic is prevalent in situations where one partner suffers from an addiction and the other repeatedly rescues or covers up for him or her. For example, the wife of an alcoholic husband frequently finds herself taking over her husband's responsibilities, whether it be paying the bills, raising the children (and all that that entails), taking care of the house, bailing him out of embarrassing situations—including jail—and socially covering up for him. The wife's life becomes unmanageable as she fails to tend to her own needs. As for the husband, there is no reason for him to change—everything is taken care of for him, and he suffers few of the consequences of his addiction.

Those fortunate enough to find help in 12 Step programs soon learn that they have absolutely no power to change their loved one's self-destructive ways, and that their own lives will improve, often dramatically, when they begin to focus on addressing their own shortcomings, including their propensity to control. When enablers finally stop trying to change their loved ones, the loved ones are compelled to endure the consequences of their own actions. Only when those consequences become "painful" enough are they motivated to seek the necessary help for their addictions.

THE LOVE CONTROL TEST

Are you a love controller? Let's find out. Ask yourself the following:

- Do I usually feel I know what's best for my partner?
- Am I often impatient with him or her?
- Do I try to solve his or her problems?
- Am I quick to point out my partner's shortcomings?
- Do I look to the other person for my own happiness?

"Yes" answers to these questions indicate you are trying to control the relationship. Now answer these questions:

- Do I listen to my partner's concerns without trying to solve them?
- Am I patient with his or her struggles?
- Do I play a part in my love conflicts?
- Do I accept my partner's annoying traits?

"Yes" answers to these questions indicate you are *not* trying to control the relationship.

LOSING LOVE CONTROL

Rita was a successful, attractive, high-energy fashion model who for years searched intensely for Mr. Right. Her agenda became more and more rigid as she sought out a man who loved skiing and kayaking, was a sharp dresser, and, most important, let her call the shots in the relationship. Any man who didn't meet these criteria was quickly dropped. Rita met a lot of men, but her relationships were short-lived because the men either did not meet her expectations or, just as often, were turned off by her attempts to mold them to suit her needs.

As the years passed and Rita hadn't found Mr. Right, time became of the essence. She was often noticeably tense and anxious and had even lost several large modeling accounts. Six months went by before I next saw her at a beach house she had rented for the summer. She had changed dramatically. She was happy and carefree, which was delightful to see. And she was dating a man whom she really liked, but who disliked outdoor sports, was a bit overweight, and had a job as a department store dresser.

"Danny," Rita shared with me, "my life has changed so much, I can't believe it. Just three months ago, I was so stressed out that I told myself, 'I can't do this anymore. No more looking, no more trying—no more men!' I just let go of everything. And would you believe it, that's when I met Jim. He just keeps me in stitches all the time, and I also got three new accounts this past month!"

"You relinquished control," I told her.

"I what?" Rita asked, a puzzled look on her face.

"You stopped pressing, and that opened the door for new things to come your way," I explained.

"Yes, that's exactly right. I did," she said, and giggled.

For Rita, losing control came through not being so relentless in her love pursuit. When she finally let go, unexpected results followed. This is the essence of *losing* love control.

The compulsion to control intimate relations is in large part driven by the belief that our happiness is dependent on others, that if our loved ones would just change or be the way we want them to be, we would be happier. Hence, the focus is on changing them rather than on changing ourselves. The folly is trying to change what is for the most part unchangeable. People will change only if they choose to, irrespective of our desires and efforts.

I leave you to ponder this question: Will changing your partner truly satisfy your own needs?

EMBRACING YOUR LOVE FEARS

If you find yourself criticizing, nagging, or otherwise complaining about your partner, try to find out whether there is some underlying fear and anxiety behind it. For example, if you get upset because your husband is always running around and doing so much that he is exhausted by the end of the day, examine the reason for your complaint. Is it that he doesn't spend enough time with you? Is it the fear that he lashes out at you over little things because he is irritable when he is tired? Likewise, if you are unsettled by your wife's pursuing her passion for art by attending week-long workshops or doing too much volunteer work, examine why. It may be that you feel a void in your own life, and your wife's activities bring that point home to you.

Conducting a simple fear inquiry in such a case (see chapter 6) will help you hone in on your fears as well as on other unwanted Personal Truths that may be impacting your love relations. Once you identify these feelings, you can begin to process them. In the first example above, you could share with your husband your fear that he will verbally abuse you when he becomes exhausted from over-activity. If he does not take stock of his unkind ways, you could detach from him at such times by doing something in another area of the home or even getting out of the house for a while. In other words, focus on taking better care of yourself. In the second example, you cannot change your wife's life choices to suit your needs, but you do have the power to do things that will make your life more fulfilling.

ACCEPTING YOUR LOVED ONE

In the final analysis, *losing* love control is best accomplished by accepting your partner for who, what, and how he or she is. You are essentially powerless over changing traits you dislike, and trying to do so only makes things worse. You are much better served by focusing on what you do have control over: your role in the relationship. Your love life will improve exponentially when you work on reducing your expectations and shortcomings and on improving your attitudes, actions, and reactions within the relationship.

CHAPTER ELEVEN

LOSING SPORTS CONTROL: *GAINING* THE COMPETITIVE EDGE

If you make every game a life-and-death thing,
you're going to have problems. You'll be dead a lot.

—*Dean Smith, basketball coach*

STAR ATHLETES LEARN EARLY on that giving up some control enhances their performance as well as that of their team. A prime example is Kobe Bryant. When Kobe started playing for the L.A. Lakers, he pressed hard to make things happen instead of allowing the action to come to him. This often resulted in poor shot selection and more turnovers. Just as important, it also prevented his teammates from effectively utilizing their own unique skills. With experience, however, Kobe learned to be more patient and wait for opportunities to unfold within the natural flow of the game so he could spontaneously utilize his special talents.

By *losing* some control, Kobe has frequently ascended to that flow zone (as all great athletes do) where he plays confidently and fluidly. And just as important, with more assists he raises his teammates' level of play as they, too, are able to participate more freely within the flow of the game. This has not gone unnoticed by other teams. Highly renowned coach Don Nelson of the Golden State Warriors complimented Kobe's new style of play in the December 30, 2008 issue of the *Los Angeles Times*: "He allows these guys to do their thing and be successful and encourages them. He makes them even better than they are by playing along side of him...and you couldn't say that five years ago. But now you can say it. That's why he is such a complete player."

In a similar vein, former L.A. Clippers coach Alvin Gentry, describing the improved play of small forward Corey Maggette, also told the *Times* (March 8, 2001), "Maggette's taking his time now. When he doesn't rush things and just allows things to happen in the flow of the game, he's always been a very good player. The only time he gets in trouble is when he forces the issue."

Kobe himself is very much aware of the results of pressing too hard. After a sub par (for him) performance in the deciding game seven of the 2010 NBA championship series with the Boston Celtics, Kobe remarked, "I just wanted it so bad...and the more I tried to push, the more it kept getting away from me." (*Los Angeles Times*, June 18, 2010).

Sports: A Hotbed of Control

Competitive sports are a hotbed of control. The intensity and pressure—and excitement—of competition propels athletes to continually press the action, even when it goes against the flow of the game. Most of the time, however, forcing the action adversely impacts performance. It causes you to tighten up, make poor decisions, and not play "your game."

In tennis, for example, swinging too hard at the ball causes you to lose your rhythm and make more unforced errors. When you smash volleys, you hit more balls out or into the net. In golf, when you swing too hard off the tee, you may look up and shank the ball. And when you overanalyze your swing, you inhibit your natural stroke. Similarly, in football, when the quarterback forces passes against tight defensive coverage, he risks interceptions. When running backs strive too hard for additional yardage, they fumble more often.

In baseball, batting slumps are prolonged when players try too hard to come out of them. Players typically take extra batting practice to no avail. They analyze their swing in great detail with the help of videos and batting coaches, trying to spot defects, then make adjustments only to become more mired in their slumps. The irony is that when they finally "give up" on their efforts (i.e., *lose* control), they start hitting the ball well again. A prime example is former L.A. Dodgers outfielder J. D. Drew. In explaining his strong spring-training start following a subpar season, he commented, "Last year I hit way too much in the cages when I was struggling and it just made it worse. This year I'm going to take minimal swings, but the right kind of swings." Drew's ability to know when to "let go" resulted in his making the American League All-Star Team.

MARK: FROM "OVERCOACH" TO COACH

Mark played basketball from early childhood through high school and loved it. He learned the benefits of letting go of control in coaching when he took on the job of shepherding the sixth-grade girls' basketball team at the school where he teaches.

At practice, he focused on teaching the game's basic fundamentals to his players, using diagrams and a chalkboard to show them how to set plays. However, what he taught in practice didn't carry over to the games. The pressure and excitement of the games caused the girls to play in a freewheeling style in which they made numerous turnovers. Mark constantly harped on them to slow down and set up plays, but to no avail. The more the girls tried to follow his instructions, the worse they played. In particular, his star player stopped improvising and doing what she did best.

Mark's team lost most of their games the first two seasons. He was frustrated and discouraged, and so were his players. When I visited with him a year later, he was very upbeat about the upcoming season. His third season as coach had been his most successful. When I asked Mark what had changed, he replied: "I realized that I had been overcoaching, and that hurt our team's performance."

"What do you mean?" I asked.

"Well," he said, "I learned that my job was to try to teach and prepare the team the best way I could, but when the game started, I needed to just let them play. Trying to instruct them too much during the game simply didn't work. They played much better when I just encouraged and supported them in a positive manner, asking them to make only slight adjustments here and there. They ended up having more fun and winning more games. And the funny thing about it is, they actually applied more of what I had taught them when I stopped prodding them so much."

Losing control in sports and competition maximizes performance. It enables you to play within yourself and the natural flow of the game as it continually evolves. You have a greater overview of the game as it progresses and can make effective changes in strategy. Also, when you let the game come to you, rather than you to the game, you can apply your skills and talents more effectively. You can adapt and adjust to momentum swings. At the same time, you enhance the "ensemble" play of your teammates, as everyone feeds off one another.

LEARNING TO LET GO

I have enjoyed sports and been a competitive athlete since I was a young child. Through the years I have learned certain basic practices and principles that enhance performance. All involve an aspect of *losing* control.

1. MAINTAIN REALISTIC EXPECTATIONS

Don't expect too much of yourself. Overly high expectations raise the stakes and increase the pressure, resulting in controlling actions. You tend to press too much and not recognize changes that will improve your performance. You may not notice weaknesses in your opponent's game that you could capitalize on. If you are not performing at your best, don't put too much emphasis on it. We all have bad days. Sometimes our body just doesn't do what we want it to. We may have other things on our mind that distract us. Remember this: a bad day or week doesn't mean a bad player or bad career!

Also, undue expectations taken to the extreme can result in serious injuries by asking the body to do too much. A good case in point is that of Liu Xiang, who became a national sports icon after being the first Chinese athlete ever to win a track-and-field gold medal, in the 110-meter hurdles at the 2004 Olympic Games in Athens. The pressure was high for him to repeat at the 2008 Olympic Games in Beijing. Unfortunately, Liu seriously injured his Achilles tendon during training for the Games and was unable even to compete in the first qualifying heat of his event.

It is thus important to maintain realistic expectations. Goals are fine, but make them reasonable. Think in terms of performing well rather than great and of enjoying the game instead of pressing too hard. Perfection is not for us mortals.

2. STAY WITHIN YOUR GAME

When playing against a stronger team or player, it is very easy—and natural—to try to compensate by doing too much. Invariably, however, this compels you to play outside your natural comfort and skill zone. I have experienced this firsthand many times when I am playing doubles in tennis and my partner is having an off day. My inclination is to take control and try to do too much. I serve harder than I should, try too hard to make a perfect shot, and go after balls that are beyond my reach—becoming very tired in the process—all of which lead to more errors. It also takes my partner even more out of his game. I now know that it is better for me to keep playing my normal game and just offer encouragement to my partner.

The same often happens when the best players on weaker teams play superior opponents. On numerous occasions I have witnessed a star basketball player make poor shot selections, not pass to open players, and otherwise try to do too much. I have seen the same thing happen with star soccer players. Their controlling ways impact the game of their teammates by effectively keeping them out of the game.

In a similar vein, when a skilled boxer in a championship title fight tries to become a puncher against a heavy-hitting puncher, the usual result is that the skilled boxer ends up on the deck.

Hence, it is better to stay within your own game and unique skills. Avoid pressing and trying to do too much, too soon, or too different. Just be patient and wait for things to open up for you, then apply your talents within a framework that optimizes your performance—and your results.

3. ACCEPT "WHAT IS"

In every sport, you have good moments and bad moments, good breaks and bad breaks. The important thing is to know which you have the power to change and which you don't. If you are a quarterback and have thrown some pass interceptions, accept that it is part of the game and don't dwell on it; just focus on the next play. Otherwise, you may press and make more bad passes. Similarly, if you are a basketball player who has missed several three-pointers, don't get down on yourself or become too cautious. That only results in more missed shots. Instead, focus on the fundamentals of your shot. If you play baseball and have struck out twice, let that be and focus on keeping your eye on the ball.

All too often, athletes dwell on trying to change things over which they have absolutely no control. For example, you can't change double faults in tennis, missed field goals in football, bogies in golf, wild pitches in baseball, or blown layups in basketball. Nor can you change the way your teammates are playing by scolding or chiding them. When your teammates aren't playing well, trying to correct them rarely helps; instead, it often hurts by increasing the pressure they already feel. Such negative energy can only adversely impact the team's performance.

In short, the more you can accept the circumstances, the more you can let go of control.

Greater success in sports comes from changing the things you can. You can change your reactions and attitudes. You can encourage and support teammates who are having a bad game. You can be less critical of your own performance. You can choose to have more fun. When you make mistakes, you can identify the causes and try to avoid repeating them by focusing on basic fundamentals. In tennis, when I make errors I remind myself to get ready for the ball earlier, improve my footwork, focus on the ball, or perhaps change my strategy.

4. EMBRACE YOUR PERSONAL TRUTHS

Competition and performance of all kinds, sports and otherwise, invoke strong emotions (Personal Truths), particularly anger, anxiety, and fear of failure. This is not easy to do, but when you are able to embrace these powerful feelings, the competitive tension and anxiety ease, allowing you to play and perform more within the rhythm and flow of the game.

Even if you cannot embrace these feelings, just being aware of their existence helps. It brings them to the surface, where they can be viewed as simply feelings and not facts. This defuses them. For example, if you are feeling tense and nervous before an important game or event, try to identify its source. More often than not, it will be fear based. Perhaps it is the fear that you will embarrass yourself or let your teammates down. Next, try to get in touch with the fear. A good way is through simple meditation or deep breathing, wherein you focus on and try to feel the fear itself. Is your chest or stomach tight? If so, breathe into that area and feel the physical sensations. Stay with them. The tension and anxiety will diminish and you will begin to relax and feel calmer.

You can also do a worst-case scenario exercise by asking yourself a series of what ifs: What if I don't play well? How important is that? Is a bad day going to ruin my life? Am I going to be kicked off the team? Will it stop me from playing well the next game? And so on. Such questions help you gain perspective and thereby reduce your anxiety because you will realize that not nearly as much is at stake as you feared.

5. VISUALIZE PERFORMING WELL

Visualizing performing well can be extremely beneficial. I have found it helpful to visualize in two basic ways. The first is to visualize letting go and getting in touch with a smooth rhythm and flow at the very start of the competition. Just close your eyes and picture yourself performing smoothly and staying within your basic game plan. Try to see yourself moving in an easy and confident manner. Stay with the images until they become fertile in your mind. Repeat them right up to the time the competition starts so that they carry over to the game itself. Before an important tennis match, I picture myself moving smoothly around the court—almost dancelike—and feeling light on my feet. I see myself playing confidently and utilizing my skills effectively. I also picture my opponent's style of play and effectively adapting to it.

The second visualization is more specific. Again, using tennis as an example, I picture myself turning my shoulders when I draw back the racket and then weighting forward as I stroke the ball. I let the ball roll off my fingertips when I toss it up on serves. I keep my feet active to improve my footwork. I even envision playing out actual points and, finally, winning the match.

These kinds of visualization are helpful with any sport. In basketball, you can picture yourself releasing your shot smoothly with proper arm extension or blocking out for rebounds or maintaining good balance and footwork on defense. In soccer, you can visualize yourself making accurate touch passes to your teammates or driving the ball into the far corner of the net. In golf, you can visualize keeping your head down as you rotate your hips and drive through the ball and stroking your putt smoothly toward the hole. In competitive swimming, you can visualize getting off the blocks fast and "long," and streamlining as you come off flip turns.

By using these tools for letting go of control, not only will you enhance your performance, but just as important, you will enjoy the game much more.

CHAPTER TWELVE

LOSING CREATIVE CONTROL: *FREEING* THE FLOW

It seems that the creative faculty and the critical faculty cannot exist together in their highest perfection.

—*Thomas Babington Macaulay, "On John Dryden"*

I BEGAN PAINTING AS an adult. My formal instruction consisted of only two instructional sessions with Paul Eventoff, a highly accomplished artist and friend whose work I had collected. To my vast surprise, within several years after I started, my works brought accolades. I was very encouraged by the praise I received. Because I enjoyed working outdoors, I decided to expand my knowledge of plein air painting principles and techniques by taking a weeklong fall workshop in Vermont given by some nationally known artists. I had a different instructor each day, and each one shared his or her knowledge, methods, and essential principles of landscape painting. It was total art immersion. I returned from the workshop overwhelmed but excited by all that I had been taught.

However, my excitement quickly turned to despair as I attempted to apply what I had learned. Nothing turned out right. All the new painting principles flooded my mind, but few made it to the canvas. As I pressed to work through my difficulties, the results showed no improvement and my frustration mounted. To make matters worse, I had "lost" my unique personal style.

After six months, I called Paul and related my dilemma. He shared with me the parting advice given to him by the dean of the Maryland Institute of Art upon Paul's graduation: "Now forget everything you learned and just paint!" Those words rang so true to me. I had become so controlling in trying to follow "the rules" that I had lost my sense of the freedom of the creative process itself. I had held on and held tight, and by doing so lost the joy of painting. I then decided to just paint, without any expectations. I tried to do what felt right and natural for me, incorporating my new knowledge selectively and intuitively rather than intentionally. In a few months, my painting took on a new maturity.

The key point is that each of us has our own creative nature—our unique talent, style, and way of working—and we must honor and trust that individuality. It is a vital part of who we are, and we need to embrace and remain true to it not only in the arts but also in all aspects of our lives.

HOW CONTROL IMPEDES THE CREATIVE PROCESS

Control inhibits the creative process, whether it be art, design, writing, music, dance, song, or even cooking and gardening because controlling actions restrict freedom of thought, of process, and of motion, and ultimately the connection with one's soul center. Creativity flourishes with "opening up," whereas control closes it down. We must learn to give up creative control in order to fulfill our creative potential.

Undue expectations and fear of both failure and success can make you press when a creative piece is not ready to be finished, procrastinate when you need to just dive in, overanalyze when you need to keep things simple, and obsess when you should just trust the process itself. Moreover, these obstructions can seemingly come from out of the blue. A work that is flowing smoothly can suddenly come to a screeching halt for no apparent reason. Writer's block is a good example of this. The same occurs in visual art, acting, dancing, and musical composition. The hours I have spent analyzing and overworking a painting in an effort to get it to read "right" would have been much better spent on beginning a fresh one. I have now learned to accept that certain paintings are not meant to be completed—at least the way I would like them to. I accept that they may have inherent weaknesses in design and composition, or that I lack the technical skill and experience to finish them. The reason is not as important as knowing when to stop pursuing something that is not there.

Speaking of which, there is a reason this book took over twenty years to write. Whenever I pressed to complete important passages, I stumbled, which was very disconcerting after getting off to a fast, easy start. The more I tried to push through, the more rigid my writing became. I also lost my joy and enthusiasm for writing. After a while I realized that at different times I lacked the wisdom and life experiences to go further with the material. So I would stop writing—sometimes for over a year at a time—resuming when stimulated by fresh insights and the wisdom gained from further life challenges and experiences. I learned that unlike water from a spigot, creativity does not flow on demand. And all of our persistence, analysis, and judgment are counterproductive precisely because they are so controlling. That is why I knew and accepted very early on that this book could not be completed in any manner other than that which would convey the spirit and essence of what I felt and deeply believed.

LOOSENING THE REINS

As you begin to loosen the reins, the creative process becomes highly enriching—even spiritual, for many—as freedom and openness of ideas and process seamlessly gel with knowledge and technique to produce original works of beauty and meaning. At such moments the artist is truly united with his or her core being. Some artists, as well as athletes, refer to this as "being in the Zone."

Creativity has its own natural ebb and flow, which varies day to day and moment to moment. It is important to be in touch with these creative waves and let them be your guide. For example, you may start a piece of art or writing with a burst of creative energy, and after a while it becomes only a trickle. At such times you must let go and move on, lest you lose what you already have.

KEENAN GETS INTO THE ZONE

Keenan was a fine arts major at a branch of the University of California who was gifted with a strong artistic vision. However, executing that vision was another matter altogether. His visions were so clear to him that he proceeded with impassioned intensity, often finding himself frustrated midway through because his work did not conform to his original idea.

On one such occasion when Keenan was working with clay, his teacher suggested that he stop working on his intended piece and just have fun playing with the material. Keenan did just that and soon found himself engrossed in the tactile pleasure of moving the clay around in his hands—squeezing, smoothing, pressing, twisting. He later described it to me as childlike. Then he shared with me a totally unexpected but remarkable occurrence that followed: "As I was molding the clay into different forms, at one point I saw the image of a man's face—strange and off center, to be sure—and then an idea suddenly came to me. I started breaking off pieces of the clay and molding them into all kinds of small faces. But that wasn't all. I had an old tree stump lying around in my studio to which I had inserted about thirteen leftover strands of metal from some previous metal sculpting work I had done. I affixed my little clay faces to the metal strands, and I suddenly had this really cool sculpture combining these various elements."

LOSE YOUR INTENSITY

As in Keenan's case, when you work on an art piece with too much intensity or for too long, your artistic vision can easily become very narrow. There are things you don't "see," including the broader vision of the piece. That is why visual artists will tell you that when they put a work away for weeks or months and then bring it out again, they readily note the compositional or other deficiencies. To reduce the intensity, consider taking breaks. Take a walk and get some fresh air. For me, exercise is a highly effective way of restoring my creative juices. Or, as Keenan did, just have fun!

DIVERSIFY

It is easy to stay too long with a work and end up overworking it or just getting stuck. Think about moving to another work or creative arena. It often enhances both creative endeavors. Hence, if you are not making progress writing a musical composition, work on another. If you are an actor, learn a new monologue. If you are a textile designer, look at new fabrics and materials. If you are a writer, sketch out the scene you are describing.

ALL THINGS IN MODERATION

Overly high hopes and expectations easily result in creative control. If you make the stakes too high, you are prone to press too much. Artists love to share those wonderful "accidents" that unexpectedly occurred while they were creating a work. These occur more frequently when your expectations are not high.

Maintaining realistic expectations becomes more difficult when your work has a masterful beginning. If your piece begins on a high note, try not to think about and analyze it too much. Instead, take a few moments to be grateful for your wonderful beginning and appreciate your talent, and then moderate your expectations of the finished piece.

To practice lowering expectations, take contrarian actions by creating something with the specific intention of throwing it away or not completing it. Very interesting things can happen. Chances are you will create more freely, resulting in a unique work. When you don't have the pressure of high expectations, you will tend to "stretch" and work out of your comfort level.

DON'T OVERTHINK

It is also important not to be too analytical. Thinking too much about what can or should be done to a work restricts its creative flow. You become cautious and reluctant to take chances. To counter overthinking, consider doing this exercise: start a work without any preconception of it. If you are playing a musical instrument or writing a musical composition, just let the notes or keys flow. If you are a painter, indulge yourself in the physical process and enjoy the freedom of applying and moving thick paint across the canvas. Whatever the medium, if something "clicks" for you at some point, go with it. You can add a little structure or definition, but not too much. Continue this process of interweaving looseness and structure. Then step back and enjoy your creation. Finally, put it aside and start another.

Another way to overcome overanalysis is to place short time limits for each session or work. Life-drawing instructors, for example, typically allow you as little as sixty seconds to do a sketch. If you are a writer, try completing an essay in ten minutes. If you are a dancer, choreograph your steps in five minutes. When there is literally no time to plan or think, your creative talents are freed.

Vary the Perspective

Still another useful way of *losing* creative control is to observe the piece from varying perspectives. For example, turn a painting upside down or sideways or look at it through a mirror, and note the different perspectives. Both the highlights and flaws pop right out at you. New insights occur as well.

Try the same thing in other creative forms by reversing the order or process. In dance, do the choreography from the end to the beginning. Try writing a short story or novel from the conclusion to the opening, or going in opposite directions from the middle. Write the final act of a play first. Do the first part of a musical arrangement last. You will find that varying the process in such ways brings freshness to the work and reduces preconceptions.

Embrace Your Personal Truths

Your Personal Truths will emerge as part of the creative process. You will have to process such "unwanted" feelings as anger, rejection, anxiety, and fear. When they are not dealt with, these feelings obstruct your creativity and take away the joy of the creative experience. Remember: our ultimate goal with creative endeavors is to allow our creative visions and expressions to rise from our true core.

BOWIE IS BLOCKED

Bowie was fearful about not meeting a deadline imposed by an important client who had commissioned him to compose a musical score for a new theatrical production. The more he pressed to complete the score on time, the less satisfied he was with the results. As the deadline approached, Bowie soon became overwhelmed with anxiety. He was unable to sleep nights and unable to continue. We talked about his dilemma.

"Try to separate your disabling feelings from the reality," I suggested. "What will happen if you miss the deadline?"

"My client will be very upset," Bowie quickly responded.

"What would you do then?"

"I would explain that I tried my best to deliver a really good composition, but I just need more time to complete it," Bowie said.

"What if your client says he can't wait any longer?" I probed.

"He would probably let me go and find someone else, and I would be out the money," he answered dejectedly.

"What would you do then?"

"I would have to look for other commissions."

"What if you can't find one?"

"When I look back, I've been pretty fortunate and have usually found other work, so I'm not too worried about that," Bowie said, his mood lightening.

Quizzing Bowie still more, I asked, "But what if you can't find another commission right away?"

He paused for a moment. "Well, I guess I would have to go back to being a handyman. There's always a need for a good one!" he joked. "Besides, I could use a little break."

Granted, the uncertainty Bowie faced was not easy for him, but the worst case he could imagine was not nearly as precarious as being stopped in his tracks by his fears. Bowie did lose the commission, but he didn't have to go back to using a hammer and saw. He quickly found other music assignments.

It takes courage to confront your fears and other debilitating feelings, but if you can, you will be rewarded. As those feelings subside, your anxiety will ease, your spirit will lighten, and your creative juices will begin to flow again.

PART IV

RELINQUISHING CONTROL AT WORK

CHAPTER THIRTEEN

LOSING WORK CONTROL

Work and thou canst not escape the reward:
whether thy work be fine or coarse, planting corn
or writing epics, so only it be honest work, done to
thine own approbation, it shall earn a reward to the
senses as well as to the thought.

—*Ralph Waldo Emerson, lecture before the
Society in Armory Hall, 1844*

ONE OF MY FIRST real estate investments was an older
Safeway market in Reno, Nevada, together with an unat-
tached, poorly maintained office building that had a vacant
rear lot. We purchased the property at a low price from
an elderly couple anxious to unload it. I felt there was an
opportunity to upgrade the office building and increase its
occupancy and rents, as well as possibly sell off the rear lot.
I was aware it was situated in a low-income area, but I failed
to recognize at the time that the neighborhood was rapidly
deteriorating.

To put it bluntly, our investment plans fizzled from the
get-go. Our upgrades to the office building did little to improve its occupancy. Things took a dramatic turn for the

worse when we lost key tenants after repeated burglaries, one of which involved a police shootout and the death of a robber—and front-page headlines in the local newspaper. Shortly thereafter, Safeway closed that market. To stave off foreclosure by our lender, we filed a Chapter 11 bankruptcy proceeding, which allowed us to continue to operate the property while I tried to turn it around.

I pressed hard to find new tenants by lowering rents and offering large broker commissions. When that failed, I stopped "holding on" and accepted that we had a "marked" property. I reined in my ego, which was the hardest part, and put the property on the market at a low sale price. However, even after considerable advertising and marketing efforts, the best offer we received—and a flimsy one at that—would have resulted in a 75 percent loss of our investment.

Then the tide turned in an unexpected manner. I had met a local real estate agent who was a member of a well-known national charitable organization. As it so happened, his organization was seeking to establish a shelter/work-training program in Reno. Its leaders thought the vacant food market possibly could be converted to serve that purpose and the office building could be used for its state administrative offices. The organization made a cryptic two-page offer to purchase the market and office building, subject to numerous contingencies and approvals by its multilayered divisions. Moreover, they offered a mere $500 deposit (unheard of in commercial real estate) for a one-year escrow.

My past rigid, closed-minded, controlling ways would normally have moved me to say "No way." I would never have let anyone tie up one of my properties for so long with nothing at risk. However, this time was different. I let go of preconceived notions and my prevalent control propensities and became the easiest person in the world to deal with—even though that meant using our remaining cash reserves to subsidize the property during the long escrow period. I agreed to every extension and modification the buyer requested and patiently waited until the proposed purchase proceeded through seemingly endless levels of approvals. I didn't pressure or meddle. I simply waited and waited and waited.

And then we got the bad news. The purchase had been rejected by the organization's regional board of directors. In the past, my anger would have gotten the best of me and I would have found some way to retaliate. This time, though, I did not take the decision personally. By not being so controlling, I had the vision to see that the outnumbered local office had wanted to proceed but had been unable to persuade its regional board. I thereupon supplied the local board with relevant demographic information (income and poverty levels, etc.) that could assist them in drumming up more support.

Not long after, the regional board reversed its earlier decision and voted to proceed with the purchase on an all-cash basis. Escrow closed in two weeks. A year later, the organization purchased the rear lot. We ended up making a handsome profit on the investment instead of suffering a huge loss.

THE COMPULSION TO
CONTROL AT WORK

The workplace is where humanity's primal drive for sustenance and survival is most prominently played out. As such, it is a hotbed for costly and inefficient control practices. Some graciously refer to the compulsion to control at work as just "trying to get ahead" or "make ends meet," but in truth it can be argued that it is nothing less than survival of the fittest. In certain ways, the scavenger and plunderer of primitive times has evolved into the "breadwinner" of today.

Fear once again is at the forefront of this powerful compulsion. Employers must constantly be vigilant, for who knows what dangers lurk out there—new competitors, whistle-blowers, better products, theft of trade secrets, and the like. Similarly, workers fear demotions, layoffs, and loss of benefits. And both fear the other will not respond fairly if key issues and concerns are addressed forthrightly. Hence, we find employees quitting without adequate notice and employers firing without prior warning.

THE INEFFICIENCIES OF
WORK CONTROL

When we are rigid in our way of doing things, we prevent ourselves from adapting to changing circumstances and priorities, as well as recognizing viable options. There is thus little room for creative improvisation. There are no quarterback options, either. Moreover, we tend to become headstrong when the currents don't flow our way. Our interactions become abrasive and confrontational instead of cooperative and thoughtful. Consequently, more frequent and greater mistakes are made, opportunities are lost, productivity is diminished, and stagnancy prevails.

I want to be clear that I am not saying there is no room or justification for control in the workplace. To the contrary, control is necessary in establishing and maintaining efficient work practices and policies, technical procedures, quality control, and proper supervision of workers and projects, and in keeping on top of things in general. My point is to make the important distinction between needed control and guidance in the workplace and what is all too often excessive or domineering forms of control. This is often a difficult balancing act between the two, but better awareness of the harms of excessive control assists greatly in the determination.

THE BENEFITS OF *LOSING* WORK CONTROL

Cynthia, a successful casting executive at a top movie studio, prides herself on being able to uncover "real talent" from the multitudes seeking to be cast in films. In her role, she makes the initial casting decisions from pools of talent, and thereafter the actors' agents and the studio's attorneys step in to negotiate the terms of the contracts, including financial deal points and screen tests.

Cynthia related to me her mounting frustration in meeting a deadline, which was the start date of shooting a major film sequel at her studio. Early on she had chosen fine actors for the leading roles, but the attorneys and agents kept bickering over the contract negotiations. In particular, several of the agents were refusing further screen testing for their clients. Cynthia shared with me that she was growing more and more anxious because of the constant delays and felt hamstrung by her inability (by industry practice) to become directly involved in the negotiations. Instead, she kept pushing from the sidelines with no success.

Finally, after a costly five-week delay in the start date of the movie, she told me that she had said to herself, "I've become too emotionally vested in this. I'm done, I've done everything I can, it's a fair deal," and walked away from the situation. After that, she said, everything fell into place. The contracts were finalized and the cameras began rolling.

Cynthia's story shows that there is a less stressful way of working and doing business. When you are able to give up some control to the natural rhythm of work in which events progress, regress, evolve, and change in unpredictable ways, it sets the stage for new solutions, higher productivity and efficiency, fewer mistakes, and a savings of considerable time and energy.

Here are some of the specific benefits of relinquishing control in the workplace.

1. Your Vision Expands

As you *lose* control, your intensity diminishes and your blinders are removed, giving you a broader and more objective perspective of the issues at hand. Your "vision" literally expands, and you see viable avenues that previously had been obscured.

A good example is the story involving my flagship property (see chapter 2). After suffering a number of setbacks—including my unexpected surgeries—following my purchase of this office building, I decided to mentally let go and stop "working" the property. This action removed the blinders and allowed me to see options I hadn't before.

2. You Quickly Get to the Heart of Strategic Issues

When you let go of control at work, there is less "debris" that obstructs the path to realistic solutions. Greater clarity enables you to hone in on the crux of your work challenges. There are fewer diversions and blind alleys.

3. YOU MAKE FEWER MISTAKES

Because you are more flexible and adaptable when you let go of control, you can make adjustments before laboring too long on costly and unproductive tasks and ventures. You make decisions within the context of the current facts as they evolve. As a consequence, you make both fewer and less serious mistakes.

4. YOU RESOLVE COMPLEX ISSUES MORE EASILY

Losing control is particularly beneficial in complex decision making where key issues appear to have no clear or easy resolution. These are typically situations involving multiple parties with unknown or differing motives and where important information is not yet known. Such cases are prone to repeated vacillation, overanalysis, and second-guessing. In complex situations like these, letting go of control simplifies the decision-making process. When I'm faced with this, instead of fretting about possible outcomes, I try to let things unfold by themselves. I become more of an observer, patiently waiting for new information and paths to reveal themselves and then attempting to intuitively interact with them. I have come to learn that there are few situations for which there is a right or wrong way of doing things; rather, there are often diverse paths to the same goal. The key is being able to follow, with confidence and without resistance, the ones that best suit your needs, and letting go of control and trusting your intuition is the best way to accomplish that.

5. YOUR WORK BECOMES MORE ENJOYABLE

When you control less at work, there is less intensity, confrontation, and resistance. You are more centered and grounded, and you have less worry and anxiety. As the expression goes, you become "kinder, gentler" and people respond accordingly. Work becomes more enjoyable and rewarding.

6. YOUR CAREER PATH FULFILLS YOUR PASSIONS

What is particularly exciting about *losing* control at work is that it helps forge a career path that has a greater chance of fulfilling your true passions and interests. Because you are less rigid and more open, you are "available" to unplanned and unexpected opportunities and changes that frequently serve as catalysts for new ways of seeing, thinking, and doing. Even perceived adversities can lead to remarkable career benefits.

RAYMOND: FROM COMPOST TO THE CLASSROOM

Take the case of Raymond, for example. Over many years Raymond, a small businessman, used hard work and perseverance to build up his compost and fertilizer business. At one point he supervised a dozen employees and had seven large trucks transporting his product to construction and home sites. Though he enjoyed owning his own business, he certainly did not enjoy the smell. As he was fond of saying, it was a "s***ty" business, and he had tons of the stuff.

Business slowed dramatically for Raymond in the recession of the early 1990s. He made cutbacks where he could, but over a two-year period things got progressively worse until he was on the brink of bankruptcy. Raymond was frightened and depressed, and he did all he could to hold on to his failing business. The last straw was an eviction notice from his landlord. That was when he knew he had to let go. He had thirty days to get out and have the "stuff" moved out of the site. After a herculean effort, he managed to haul all of it out, and was left with no business and no idea what to do with his life.

Well into his fifties, Raymond, with nothing but time on his hands, on a lark decided to take elementary teacher certification courses at a local college. Several years later he was working at different elementary schools as a substitute teacher. Raymond's entire life had changed. Never having had children of his own, he experienced for the first time the joy and innocence of young children. Work was no longer a burden but something he eagerly looked forward to every day. Raymond had unexpectedly found his passion, and he found it by letting go of control.

How to *Lose* Work Control

The basic principles for relinquishing control at work are similar to those for giving up control in other areas of your life. One of the most important principles is accepting the "what is" of the workplace, whether it be declining profits and compensation, disgruntled co-workers, unpleasant bosses and work assignments, and the like. By accepting such realities, you don't lose time and energy—and serenity—trying to change things over which you have little control. Instead, you can examine what you do have the power to change, such as your attitude, expectations, and work practices. This will both minimize the hardships and bring you more peace of mind.

Another important principle for letting go of control is acknowledging and processing your Personal Truths—particularly the fears, frustrations, and anger that arise almost daily in dealing with work challenges and issues.

For me, in one particular case, my being able to accept "what was" brought unexpected success. A real estate agent had placed a large, unauthorized "For Sublease" sign at the entrance to one of my properties. I had known and done business with this agent for over twenty years. He knew we never allowed such signage. Furious, I was ready to take legal action.

Fortunately, I didn't. Instead, I worked at processing my anger and hurt feelings. Then I asked myself how important this "affront" really was. I recognized that the only real harm was to my feelings, not to the property. I told the agent that my feelings were hurt and asked if he was resentful of me for some reason. He said no, he simply felt he had a duty to represent his client, the sublessee, and that duty took precedence over my interests. I could at least understand the basis for what he did, even if I disagreed with it. As my anger subsided, I was able to accept "what was" and allowed the sign to remain without losing any sleep over the incident, which was a far cry from what I would have done earlier in my career.

Several days later, someone called the agent and asked to look at the sublease space. The caller decided the space did not suit his needs but did find another space in our building that he liked. This new tenant later told me that he would never have stopped to look at the space in our building had it not been for the unauthorized sign. Wow! Who would have known? Certainly not me.

I have experienced time and again that when I am able to accept "what is," the dynamics of an unsettling situation change, often dramatically. Positive thoughts and energy replace negative ones. Obstacles are lessened or removed. Unexpected paths appear. It is not unlike "making peace, not war."

PATIENCE IS A VIRTUE

When my daughter Lora was young, she would always say to me, "Daddy, patience is a virtue." That wisdom holds true in so many situations, especially in the workplace. Patience keeps you from pressing and jumping ahead of work's natural currents. By showing restraint, you can wait for events to unfold until an opportune time arises in which to take constructive action. When you do this, your action will be more effective because it better "fits" the circumstances at hand.

Learning to be patient in most instances requires that you confront your fears. It is our fears that usually compel us to take precipitous action. Therefore, when you are having difficulty being patient, do the exercises on conducting a fear inquiry and confronting fear, as described in chapter 6.

I am fully aware that it is hard to be patient in certain situations, such as when you are under severe financial pressure. At bottom, it requires that you have trust and faith that you will be okay regardless of what happens— and trust and faith that you are doing the right thing by doing "nothing" (or going more slowly) so that you can better observe and evaluate the situation.

I have observed a valuable trait present in most successful businesspeople: they are almost always willing to let a deal go if they can't get the terms and safeguards they desire, and they are willing to step back and wait until they can get the deal they want. While these people may lose out on many more deals than they make, they make significantly fewer mistakes and rarely enter into a deal that doesn't work out well for them.

CHAPTER FOURTEEN

FOLLOWING THE PATH
OF TRUTH

Honesty is the first chapter in the book of
wisdom.

—*Thomas Jefferson, in a letter*
to Nathaniel Macon, 1819

IN COLLEGE I KNEW of someone who cheated on his exams and seemed proud of the novel ways in which he did it. He also liked to boast about how easy it was for him to steal toiletries from a store where he worked part-time. Following graduation, he appeared to carry his dishonest ways over to his business. They became so ingrained in him that his lack of integrity became business as usual. And he made millions that way, too. But he assumed that others were not smart enough to see through his schemes. He was wrong, and got caught—big time. A competitor (and friend) informed on him for illegally exporting goods. That eventually led to his being prosecuted and serving time in a federal prison.

Unfortunately, my friend does not stand alone. Business headlines repeatedly trumpet the demise of those who ignore truth and honesty in their drive to accumulate great wealth and influence. Such people foolishly believe they are more powerful than the "ocean" in which they swim, and consequently try to tame that ocean to fit their needs, rather than riding its currents to their legitimate ends.

HOW WE DIVERGE FROM THE PATH— AND HOW TO FIND OUR WAY BACK

In today's business world, there is too little regard for truth, honesty, and, yes, kindness. Indeed, truth is all too often pushed to the far corners—and in many instances out the door—as work and business ethics have taken a backseat to hubris, profit, and greed. Need I cite more than the massive financial and credit meltdown in the fall of 2008 and the astounding deceit, fraud, and abuse of trust of its underbelly?

Expediency, manipulation, and deception are prominent control mechanisms used in the drive to "succeed" at all costs. For all too many, there exists what I believe to be a double standard between how one conducts one's business affairs and how one conducts one's personal affairs. We often find businesspeople and workers being abusive, unkind, and dishonest in work matters, yet charitable and thoughtful in their personal lives. As the familiar refrain goes, "He's a mean SOB in business, but a peach of a guy personally," or "It's only business." But in truth, ethics and decency are not so conveniently divisible.

When you are not being truthful, you are controlling and manipulating people and events, thereby obstructing the natural work rhythm. You snake through winding paths: ones that consume inordinate amounts of time and energy, ones that are inefficient and unproductive, and ones that deprive you and those around you of serenity. I often wonder about the sheer amount of unproductive time that dishonest people spend in keeping up their lies and trying to be consistent in their stories. As their web of deceit expands, they have to keep track of more and more. To respond to even simple questions, they must stop and think about what they said earlier in an effort to maintain consistency, rather than respond with a truthful answer. These diversions in the end are very costly because truly productive matters cannot be pursued. In fact, the truth requires no more time or energy than simply stating it. And just think how much better it will be to sleep peacefully after that.

Being truthful includes avoiding so-called half-truths and white lies. The big problem with small falsehoods is that they multiply. Typically, people start with little lies and get away with them, even making money to boot. This makes them feel increasingly more secure in their devices, and they consequently engage in shadier practices.

Believe it or not, people are much more forgiving of truth and candor than they are of deceit. Truth diffuses, whereas concealment and deceit fuel. For example, creditors will often work with debtors who acknowledge they don't have the funds to fully satisfy their obligations. Creditors will offer these debtors a reasonable plan for repayment, as opposed to debtors who do not return calls or send checks that don't clear the bank.

A GRATEFUL TENANT

Following the chaotic events of September 11, the largest tenant in one of my buildings had a liquidity crisis resulting from a dramatic drop in sales and asked to meet with me. At the meeting, the company's CEO requested a rent abatement until his business could get back on its feet. He presented a business plan for the next year that included layoffs and other cost-reduction measures. We worked out a rent payment plan for a two-year period that included rent reductions and abatements, as well as lease extensions that benefited us.

The tenant gradually became profitable again and later leased additional space in the building, increasing both our revenues and the value of the building. When we eventually decided to sell the building, the tenant was instrumental in our obtaining a good price for it by promoting our building to prospective purchasers. Not only that, but several years later the same tenant relocated to another of my buildings, leasing almost 40 percent of it.

I firmly believe that integrity requires that you follow a Path of Truth in all realms of your life, and no less so at work and in business. The need to "get ahead" does not justify treating others wrongly. The Path of Truth empowers you and others, minimizes conflicts and distractions, and reduces stress and anxiety. It also establishes the trust and credibility that is essential for long-term success. And most important, it makes work both honorable and enjoyable.

TRUTH PRACTICES

Working in a candid, truthful manner is the only way to glide smoothly with work currents and enjoy their numerous benefits. When truth is the bottom line instead of profits, conflicts and confrontations are reduced and cooperation and support are encouraged.

Through many years of experience, I have learned that there are three straightforward but powerful Truth Practices that fluidly guide you along the Path of Truth: (1) disclose relevant facts, (2) acknowledge your mistakes, and (3) ask the hard questions.

DISCLOSE RELEVANT FACTS

Following the Path of Truth doesn't just mean affirmatively stating the truth. It also includes timely disclosure of relevant facts and information to which the parties involved are entitled to know. When you conceal such information in an attempt to control the outcome, it usually results in a worse outcome. People are entitled to make informed work and business decisions about what concerns them. They can be very unforgiving when they learn about unfavorable information after the fact.

Full disclosure is a way of letting go of control. Rather than spending valuable time trying to restrict or withhold information, disclosure allows events to take their natural course.

I know this firsthand. As a real estate attorney and professional investor, I counseled affluent investors about their failed investments. Most either had not received full information at the inception or had not been informed about their investments' poor performance. Most were resentful when they finally learned the true facts. Lawsuits sometimes ensued. In many cases, much of the bitterness could have been avoided had the promoters disclosed the unfavorable information in a timely manner.

In short, if the waters become infested with sharks, you have a duty to tell the others swimming with you. Proper disclosure of risks and unfavorable information enhances credibility and confidence. People know that not everything is a bed of roses. They just want to know where the thorns are so they can better protect themselves against getting pricked. That's why the trustworthy navigator gets more passengers.

It is also important to be timely in your disclosures. Some people fess up after it is too late to take remedial action. Although the truth can be very unsettling, wrath can be soothed by timely disclosure and often forms a common ground for effectively dealing with the problem.

The flagship property I described in chapter 2 illustrates the benefits of full disclosure. I was so enthusiastic about the prospects of the investment that I invested a substantial amount myself. The purchase price was low because of the building's high vacancy rate, but I was confident that could be overcome with better management and planned building upgrades.

However, several weeks following the purchase of the property, medical difficulties put me out of commission during the critical ownership transition. To make matters worse, this occurred during an office building boom in which there was severe competition. At one point there was more than a five-year supply of office space on the market. To counter that, I lowered rates, upgraded the building, and advertised extensively—but to no avail.

I then made a very difficult but important decision. I informed my investors in detail of the unanticipated adversities, which I knew would come as a surprise to many of them because it came so soon after our purchase of the property. I also detailed the efforts I was making to overcome our problems and followed that with regular status reports. Only several of the investors expressed dissatisfaction. Most were supportive and appreciative that I had informed them of the problems at an early juncture.

As I mentioned in chapter 2, two of my investors even offered to help. They flew with me to Utah to meet with the seller, a well-known industrialist who was also our lender. With their help, a settlement was reached that enabled us to extricate ourselves from the investment without losing our shirts. Hence, had I not disclosed the negative information to my investors, I am certain we would have lost all our money.

My act of disclosure was a way of *losing* control and following the Path of Truth under difficult circumstances. All my efforts in trying to overcome the investment's obstacles were for naught. Nothing had worked. Only when I accepted the fact that I was powerless over the adversity did a solution come forth. And notably, when I visited the building twenty years later, it was still substantially vacant.

People are entitled to know of adversities that impact them. They should be given the opportunity, even if remote, to try to remedy their situation. They may be upset, but they will likely respect you for being candid with them. Also, by keeping the truth from others, you deprive yourself of input that could possibly lead to viable solutions to seemingly insolvable problems.

ACKNOWLEDGE YOUR MISTAKES

Trust takes considerable time to earn but very little time to lose. Acknowledging your mistakes greatly enhances trust and credibility. It allows you to move beyond defensive posturing. Moreover, by acknowledging your mistakes and oversights, your actions and statements will be viewed as being more truthful and thus have greater impact, whether in strategic negotiations or regular job duties.

Yet, many people refuse to acknowledge their mistakes at work. Some even go to great extremes to conceal them. They fear the unknown and feel vulnerable and exposed.

These people lack confidence in others' willingness to forgive and understand. Keep in mind that most people do not expect perfection. There is much truth in that famous expression "To err is human."

When you conceal your mistakes, you must deal with the anxiety and stress of their being discovered. This promotes further covering up. The famous Watergate cover-up in the 1970s, which led to the resignation of a president, is a prime example. It was the huge roar and publicity of the ongoing cover-up that caused the fatal political damage, not the misdeed itself.

MY SICK MEDICAL BUILDING

Let me provide another example from my own experience, in which my admission of some serious blunders turned what would have been a financial disaster into a profitable investment. I had formed an investment partnership to purchase an older medical building in Utah for which the tenants were paying below-market rents. My investment plan was to update and refurbish the building and bring rents closer to market, thereby increasing its value. However, we embarked on the program without first getting to know our tenants well and informing them of the improvements we planned for the building.

Many of the tenants were very upset by the rent increases from their out-of-state owners. They called a tenant meeting and, in short order, we had a major tenant revolt on our hands. Some even threatened to leave. In medical buildings, if you lose a key doctor or two, others usually follow because they rely on patient cross-referrals.

I had made a serious mistake and knew it. We had lost credibility with our tenants. To them, we were money-mongers who showed no interest or concern for their needs.

I felt compelled to do something dramatic to avoid becoming the proud owner of an empty building! I decided to surprise the tenants by painting the entire building with what I thought were very appealing colors. (I even consulted with a professional designer in selecting the colors.) I felt this gesture would reassure the tenants that we had their best interests at heart.

To my astonishment, the gesture backfired. The doctors were angrier than ever. They were furious that I hadn't consulted with them in selecting the color for their building. They liked the previous drab color better.

I was really in a quandary—and obsessed with worries and "what ifs." What if the tenants left en masse? How would we make our mortgage payments? What would I tell my partners?

Several days later it occurred to me that I had been very controlling. My fear and anxiety had caused me to press too hard to find a solution to the problem, and in the process I had compounded one mistake with another. Rather than act hastily again, I elected to just let things be and reflect on my mistakes. One clear error was that I had not taken into account the feelings of my tenants. I had selected a dramatic new color for "their" building without consulting them. I was viewed as an insensitive outsider who had intruded upon their home.

A plan began to emerge. I sent a personal letter to each of the doctors letting them know that I wanted to meet with them personally so that I could respond to their grievances. During a series of meetings held at the building, I apologized for my insensitivity in not having consulted with them regarding the selection of a paint color. Further, I promised to confer with them with respect to future changes to the building.

I also acknowledged that the rent increases were handled impersonally. I explained that our operating costs had increased because we were trying to maintain the building in a more professional manner than the prior owner had.

Next, I let them know how important it was to us that they remained at the building and acknowledged that their leaving would seriously jeopardize our investment and that I was aware they had space options at other buildings. At this point in the meetings there was a noticeable mood shift. By admitting my mistakes and apologizing for my insensitivity, their anger subsided and a rapport began to develop. I had taken the first steps in establishing my sincerity.

I was then able to offer valid reasons why it was in their best interests to remain at the building. I quoted studies that showed that physicians could lose up to 50 percent of their patients by moving even a short distance. I explained to them that developers in the area were making a lot of promises, particularly regarding rental rates, and they should investigate the basis of the promises carefully. For example, I advised them to verify how footage was measured or what expenses they may have to pay, so they could make accurate rent comparisons. I also told them they may end up having to pay for substantial tenant improvements at other buildings.

The tenants responded favorably. Most said they didn't want to move but were still concerned about the sizable rent increases. I then proposed a compromise. If they were willing to renew their leases for longer terms, I would phase in the rent increases over the extended terms of their leases, rather than all at once. I also offered them certain suite upgrades. The tenants were receptive to this plan. In this way, our interests began to coalesce. When in sync, our respective waves—theirs and mine—were far stronger than when they were colliding. We thus avoided the "riptides and undertows" that come with confrontation.

It turned out that 80 percent of the doctors signed new leases, and the remainder decided to stay on a month-to-month basis until they could see how well we serviced their needs. All except two of those tenants later signed leases, and those two eventually remained at our building. Not one tenant moved!

There is no question in my mind that had I not admitted my mistakes and acknowledged our vulnerability, there would have been a mass exodus from the building. From that point on, for the next fifteen years during which we owned the building, I truly enjoyed warm relations with our tenants. Moreover, if I ever needed medical or dental advice, I had twenty physicians and dentists I could call on!

Thus, when you acknowledge your shortcomings, the issues are out in the open and you can focus on correcting them in a constructive, open manner. That is why, for example, good trial lawyers frequently disclose their clients' vulnerable points, rather than leave them to be exploited on cross-examination by opposing counsel. By withholding them, their clients' strong points are dwarfed by the emotional response that comes from "hiding something."

It simply makes good business sense to admit your mistakes. You can't make them disappear, so why appear foolish trying? Accepting "what is" places you on firmer footing because it enables you to focus on what you do have the power to change.

I believe that fear (and, to a lesser extent, shame) is the main reason people are reluctant to admit their mistakes and shortcomings. As I have mentioned before, it is un-processed fear that provokes controlling and manipulative actions—and no less so when mistakes are kept concealed.

ASK THE HARD QUESTIONS

The Path of Truth shines more brightly when paved with complete and accurate information. Because material business or work information is not always readily available or may be withheld, you must make the effort to seek it out. Many times, the only way you can do this is by asking the hard questions about the matters at hand. Unfortunately, many people don't—to their later regret.

I learned early on about the pain of failing to ask the hard questions. When I was still practicing law, one of my clients offered me the opportunity to invest in a bowling alley and discotheque venture that had started out gang-busters. He explained that one of his partners wanted to sell out for personal reasons. I had done the legal work for the investment and was excited about the opportunity to participate. After all, this was right in the heyday of Donna Summer and the disco craze. Although I knew the business was straddled with a lot of debt, that didn't concern me because the discotheque was packed when-ever I had visited it, and the bowling alley had state-of-the-art equipment. Hence, I invested without asking any questions.

A couple of months later, my client called to tell me that business had slowed and additional capital was needed. He attributed it to the seasonally weak winter period when people didn't go out as often. That seemed plausible to me, so I put up the additional capital—again, without question-ing anything.

Another two months down the road, one of the other partners called me, again requesting additional capital. The reason given this time was the unusually high insurance and security costs for the discotheque. Although I was somewhat concerned this time, I still put up my share without questioning things.

When the next call for money came, a lump formed in my chest. Something was clearly awry. I finally asked why the original partner had wanted out and why the expenses were running so much higher than projected. I also asked why business at the discotheque had not increased again with the return of warm weather.

Needless to say, I didn't like the answers. The original partner had wanted out because one of the managing partners had a serious drinking problem. That same managing partner's family had also been eating most of their meals at the bowling alley restaurant and using the bowling lanes free of charge. Insurance and security costs had increased because of the rowdy conduct of the patrons. Business was off even in warmer weather because two discotheques had opened within a mile—something my client knew but failed to tell me.

I ended up losing my entire investment, which at the time was a big setback for me. But I had learned a valuable lesson. Only by asking the hard questions up front could I properly identify and assess the risks of a business venture or opportunity. There simply was no other way.

Asking the hard questions doesn't necessarily mean you have to forgo an opportunity if the answers are not to your liking. Rather, it allows you to evaluate the investment from a broader, more fully informed perspective. Sometimes adjustments and modifications can be negotiated to reduce risks to acceptable levels. For example, had I pushed for complete information from the beginning, I could have negotiated for safeguards such as having no obligation to invest more money.

Yet, when people consult with me regarding prospective business opportunities and investments, it always amazes me how reluctant they are to delve into the heart of matters by asking the obvious questions. Many choose to see only the glamour, not the inherent risks. It is almost as if no other opportunities will come their way in the future if they pass on the deal.

There are several reasons why most of us are reluctant to get to the heart of the matter. We believe we will lose out if we delay. Sometimes we do not ask key questions because we really don't want to know the answers. We are so convinced of an opportunity's potential success that we don't want to be deterred by contrary information. In other instances, we feel we might offend the people offering the opportunity if our questions are too probing. And some of us simply are embarrassed to ask.

PETER FAILS TO ASK

An attorney friend of mine, Peter, is a good example of this. Peter wanted to relocate his offices closer to downtown Los Angeles in order to be near his client base. After looking at several possible locations, he chose one that offered low rent and had good space flexibility. However, he had to sublease the offices from a large real estate company and not directly from the landlord. When I looked at the space with him, I noticed that there were quite a few empty offices in the large suite. I suggested to Peter that he inquire more about that, which he did. The answer given to him was that the company was relocating some of its personnel to other offices in the San Fernando Valley. I then encouraged Peter to contact the landlord directly and see if the company was current in their rent. If they weren't current, Peter could be evicted along with the company, even if he was paying his rent under the sublease.

Peter felt uncomfortable asking so many questions. Instead, he moved into the suite without having all the information. He had new stationery printed up, purchased a new phone system, hired employees, and in general geared up for an expansion of his law practice.

Two months later, Peter called and dejectedly told me that the real estate company (his sublandlord) had vacated all their offices overnight. He said the building was like a morgue and his clients were unsettled by it. Several weeks later he called me again, this time sounding very harassed. Peter found out that the company had not paid its rent for many months and had legally been evicted. Moreover, the owner of the building had informed him that he had to be out of his offices within one week or all his office furniture would be moved into storage. Peter was forced to vacate and pay moving and start-up costs once again because he had been reluctant to seek the truth.

You can be sure Peter didn't hesitate to ask his next landlord about everything upfront. He didn't like every answer he received, either, but this gave him a chance to address the issues before he moved in. Likewise, you should not be discouraged from seeking the truth by asking probing questions. Your job or business—as well as your finances— is an enormously important part of your life, and you are entitled to know as much as you can.

IGNORANCE IS NOT BLISS

If the answers you receive to your probing questions are not clear or complete, or are even evasive, do not fall prey to what I call the ignorance factor, which works something like this: Let's say you're evaluating a prospective work or business opportunity, and you receive very general answers to specific questions you asked, or perhaps the other party talks over your head or facilely dismisses one of your questions with something like "There's no need to worry about that, it's covered." You are left telling yourself, "Boy, am I dumb," or "What a silly question for me to have asked."

In such instances, I have learned that usually what I had thought was ignorance or lack of understanding on my part was, in reality, a reflection of my lack of confidence in my own instincts and ability. My questions had been valid but had not been answered. I just didn't have the trust in myself to recognize that.

IS HE OR SHE TRUSTWORTHY?

As the old saying goes, it is important to know whom you get into bed with! So often in business the final decision comes down to whether you feel you can trust another's integrity. If you make mistakes about a person's character, the consequences can be devastating. That's why most successful businesspeople I know, after considering the specifics of a prospective opportunity, ask themselves, "Can I trust him or her?" That's their bottom line.

AN UNWELCOME BEDFELLOW

Lack of trust was certainly at the forefront when I tried to sell a well-located older commercial building. In commercial real estate, an unqualified or unscrupulous buyer can result in inordinate delays and wasted time, as well as lost opportunities. I received several promising offers on this particular property. One of them was much higher than the others, and the buyer's agent pressed me for an affirmative response. However, I wanted to meet with the prospective buyer first. The agent said his client was extremely busy and would not be able to meet for a while. He said that since the offer met my asking price, I should accept it and then meet with the buyer. I was tempted to follow the broker's suggestion, but I declined.

A meeting was finally arranged. The buyer was an accountant who had formed a real estate investment company that relied on capital from passive investors to acquire properties. He claimed to have syndicated ten investments in the past year, raising over $50 million from his investors, and had another half dozen acquisitions in the works. His new company specialized in purchasing old buildings and refurbishing them.

Our meeting lasted only a half hour. As a syndicator myself, I was intrigued (and a little envious) about his rapid success. Most of my questions were not related to the specifics of his offer. I was curious as to how he could raise so much money and purchase so many properties in such a short span of time. I was also intrigued by how he could so quickly refurbish the properties. I knew from prior experience that rehabbing old buildings can be very time consuming not only because you never know what you might find but also because of all the red tape in dealing with government agencies.

His answers made it all sound so simple. It was almost as if we weren't in the same business. For one thing, I knew there were very specific legal requirements for fundraising, which took time to comply with. Also, because this buyer was asking for owner financing, I wanted to know about his plans for renovating the building. He said he had a separate construction subsidiary that handled the renovations, but he did not offer specifics. Well, to me that was really a non-answer. He impressed me as far too intelligent a person to purchase such a property without having some investment plans.

I concluded that this person was likely not trustworthy and elected not to sell the building to him. It was a good thing I did. I soon learned that he had not even seen the property himself. And six months later, an article appeared on the front page of the *Los Angeles Times* reporting that both state and federal regulatory agencies had stepped in and stopped his operations. It turned out that none of his investors' money had been spent on refurbishing the properties. The monies had been funneled to offshore companies and could not be accounted for.

PART V

Losing Control, *Finding* Flow

CHAPTER FIFTEEN

THE WAVE

Obsessed with Control,
We can't let go.
But shorten life's list,
The more we resist.

Relinquish,
No longer diminish.
Let things be,
Begin to feel free.

To travel this Path,
Use its new Math.
Accept and allow—
Even meow.

Look to the Waves,
Follow their Sways.
Cresting in the Wind
Nature's magic Within.

Sometimes in tandem,
Always random.
Release,
Feel the Peace.

Life's Rhythm of Truth,
Lost in Youth,
Follows no pattern, yet
Brightens Life's Lantern.

—*Danny Miller, "Life's Lantern"*

FOR ME, THE METAPHOR that comes closest to the vision of letting go of control is one of ocean waves. The mystery, randomness, and freeness of the waves closely parallel the expansive life path we have been exploring together in this book.

Think about bodysurfing through the challenges ahead. There will be a great variety of waves, some building up quickly and crashing mightily, others cresting more gradually and lasting longer. Some will simply vanish. Many will change course. We have no influence on their patterns, paths, and frequencies; we can only be patient and alert as we await them. As soon as one crests near us, we extend our arms, swim a few strokes, and glide with it. If we encounter turbulence along the way, which we often will, we can protect ourselves. I can tell you that most of the time, the ride will be unpredictable and exhilarating.

I refer to this dynamic, ongoing process as riding or going with the "Wave" because it reminds me to let go and let be. To accept and allow. The Wave has a special rhythm, a rhythm of truth. It is an expansive approach to life, as well as a catalyst for meaningful change. It has its own parlance—high and low tides, crests, ripples, undertows, and the like—which viscerally invokes its very essence. In a very real way, for me the Wave is one of life's most beautiful poems, a poem that ultimately replaces fear, worry, anxiety, and self-imposed limitations.

One way to get a sense of the Wave is to think back to when you were a child. Probably the best practitioners of the Wave are young children. To them, life is an instinctive at times almost unconscious process, unencumbered by fears, rejection, and external events. They are thus free to "play" and be lighthearted and frivolous, yet also free to express their emotions—including pain, anger, and sadness. Children are also more trusting and willing to follow their instincts, and consequently the Wave is totally natural for them.

For most adults, however, the burdens of life's external events and pressures have produced excessive fear, anxiety, anger, and resentment. These demons, together with the consequent loss of confidence, self-trust, creativity, and spontaneity, erode our childlike nature. We have difficulty staying in tune with our feelings, and our "antennae" cannot accurately detect what is happening around us and to us. We therefore are reluctant to trust our good instincts and intuition, and instead we try to control and direct events, rather than adapting to them and allowing them to take their natural course. This control pattern shortens "life's list," makes us rigid and closed-minded, and impedes our vision, creativity, and enthusiasm.

Thus, in a sense, the Wave is what's there when we don't get in our own way. We simply need to find ways to reach back and get back on it.

A Joyful Ride

The benefits of going with the Wave, whether at work or in our personal affairs, far exceed what we experience when we constantly try to control and direct the timing and rhythm of events. With the Wave, we go farther more smoothly. We discover opportunities in what we previously perceived as limitations. It opens vistas in our mind, and we begin to relax more. We aren't as tense—and this opens the window to exploring our creative talents.

Riding the Wave has revealed options for me when the doors felt closed and my spirit heavy, fostered my creative potential in exciting ways, and enabled me to experience the freshness, fullness, and vitality of life that come with a lighter spirit and more open mind. Indeed, this remarkable ride has allowed me to channel my energy and talents toward fascinating roads never before traveled and achieve balance and harmony in my life that I could not have anticipated. I have also become more flexible and less rigid, more aware and less scattered, and more thoughtful and less abrasive.

ACCESSING THE WAVE

To get a sense of how this process works, first take some time to observe the natural progression of events in your different life settings and contexts. You will note that there are certain points or times when opportunities for participating arise naturally, as if an invitation had been extended. You will also note that even the slightest influence or intervention by you or others can create large ripples, much like tossing a pebble into a pond. This dynamic is ongoing and constantly evolving. Moreover, because everyone is unique, each individual's perception of and influence on events is different. The saying "Different strokes for different folks" clearly applies. Consequently, multiple paths arise in any given situation, and how and when you engage those paths is highly intuitive and personal. There is no right way or wrong way. But there is a good way—for you—as long as you are not pressing.

Next, try taking some trial runs where the stakes are not high. At work, for example, let the day's tasks unfold by themselves. At home, let the children do their homework and study for exams in their own way. In playing sports, sense the rhythm of the game. In the arts, follow your first expressions—and impressions. When you do get involved, sense whether it feels natural or whether you are resisting or forcing the action. Keep things as simple as you can. Do not ponder too much about what you should do.

With practice, and with confidence in the process, you will begin to instinctively feel when the time is right to take action and whether that action should be gentle or decisive. You will also learn how to make appropriate adjustments along the way. Sometimes unexpected turn of events pop out of nowhere, "urging" your involvement. Conversely, there are many occasions when matters are unclear—even chaotic—and you sense that it is best to refrain. Electing to remain patiently on the sidelines until things clear up is itself a form of relinquishing control. It is thus a stop-and-go pattern—the "to and fro" of the Wave—that develops, and as long as you are not forcing matters, meaningful opportunities will at some point arise for your constructive participation.

What's particularly nice about the Wave is how quickly it works. You feel better and lighter immediately. You will know when it's working for you and how it's working for you, and you will also know when you're just treading water and when you're caught in an undertow.

TRUSTING YOUR INTUITION

Trusting your intuition is a key element to riding the Wave successfully. In making important life decisions, our minds often work overtime trying to figure out complex puzzles using pieces from different boxes. Such "mind burdens" arise from the inherent difficulty, if not impossibility, of assigning relative values to countervailing factors that are not of the same "species." For example, in our personal affairs, some factors may involve money; others, family values. Some involve health considerations; others, pleasure. Some are slanted toward your partner's interests; others, toward your children's. In our business and work affairs, the countervailing factors may be a person's competence versus his or her unwillingness to be a team player, or a person's loyalty and reliability versus his or her failure to follow through on important matters.

Our sound intuition, however, is the "master calculator" that is uniquely able to integrate and process—in ways unbeknownst to us—the pros and cons of these varied factors, enabling us to make the right decisions for us. But to effectively utilize this innate gift, we must first let go of control by embracing our Personal Truths and accepting "what is."

STEVE TRIES THE WAVE

If ever there was a man who controlled, worried, and obsessed too much, it was my good friend Steve. After immigrating to the United States from Europe with a considerable sum of money, Steve failed at four different business ventures in a three-year period. As a result, he felt compelled to make the money back (or at least some of it), or he would lose his entire life savings.

Steve was so anxious that most nights he awoke in the wee hours terror-stricken. Consequently, he was impatient and constantly pressed. Rarely did he allow events to unfold in their normal course. He was very scattered and unfocused. At the same time, Steve had so much fear about failing yet again that when he found promising opportunities he overanalyzed them and worried himself to the point where he couldn't move ahead. His world was one of "What if?" "What should I do?" and "What could happen?" He would constantly take projects to a certain point—usually the point of commitment—and then drop them.

In short, Steve was stuck and going nowhere fast.

I spoke with Steve often about the concept of the Wave and how to apply it. Steve liked the idea but said, "I don't think it will work for me. It's too slow. I really don't have the time to try it." When I asked him how long it had been since his last business venture, he answered, "Over two years," laughing as soon as the words were out of his mouth. He immediately saw the irony of his situation. He felt the need to act fast, yet he couldn't get untracked.

He decided to give the Wave a try. "Where do I start?" he asked.

"What are your interests?" I began.

"Real estate," he told me, "but I have no real experience in it. I think I would be good at it, though, particularly the management aspects, because of my background in restaurant management."

"Why not start by taking some real estate classes?" I offered. "You can also start looking at real estate just to get your feet wet. Call on some newspaper ads and take a look at some properties. But don't stop pursuing other business opportunities that may come your way." I suggested this because I felt he would feel less pressure to push things too quickly.

Steve was game. He enrolled in a real estate investment class through a local university extension program and at the same time started looking into a variety of real estate projects to acquaint himself with the local market. He enjoyed his class and learning more about the local market. In fact, he found several promising properties and made acquaintances with local real estate professionals. He found he had a keen interest in industrial real estate.

"I'm starting to come across some pretty good deals," he told me during one of our meetings. "In fact, most of the ones that I thought were good but didn't move on sold quickly. I feel ready to do something now, but I'm worried about finding the money to complete the purchase."

"First things first," I replied. "If the deal is good enough, the money usually can be found. You're sidetracking yourself by worrying about something that doesn't exist right now. 'What ifs' aren't real. You can only ride today's currents, and that means taking the first step: tying down a good deal. Worrying about future ripples will only deter you."

Throughout the process we talked about visualizing real waves, and that had a very calming effect on Steve. His anxiety lessened and he started allowing his dealings to take their natural course. Whenever he worried that things weren't moving fast enough and started to press again, I reminded him to just "float" a while and wait for things to open up, and that it was important to wait for the right moment. It would come, and he would know when it did. In the parlance of the Wave, if you swim too fast, you may bypass an opportune current.

After a few months, things did start to come Steve's way. He purchased a piece of commercial land with two other individuals who put up most of the money. (His worries about raising the money had proved unnecessary.) He then obtained a zoning variance that allowed construction of a larger building and was able to resell the land at a substantial profit six months later. Following that, he purchased (with the same investors) two industrial buildings that he upgraded and raised the rents on, and eventually sold them at a good profit.

Several years later Steve returned to Europe, where he continued his real estate investing with even greater success. "I just go with the Wave" was Steve's motto after that. He was soon making over a half million a year—not to mention worrying a lot less and sleeping a lot better.

For Steve, the Wave began as a gradual change that became increasingly more productive for him as he witnessed its positive results. His self-confidence returned, and he stopped second-guessing himself. He learned that when he stayed out of his own way, unexpected opportunities opened up.

OBSTRUCTIONS TO THE WAVE

As you learn to ride the Wave, it is not uncommon to do well for a while and then, for no apparent reason, falter. Do not be discouraged. External events induce fear, anger, and other unwanted feelings, and our response is typically control-driven behavior that halts the flow.

The dynamic is akin to when you first learned to swim. When you entered the water, you had considerable fear and anxiety. You would swim only a few feet and then stop, even though you were doing well. These interruptions, however, became less frequent as you realized how well your newly learned strokes worked. Finally, you gained enough confidence and trust to know that you could remain afloat regardless of the obstacles you encountered. The same is true with riding the Wave. Your regressions become shorter and shorter as your trust and confidence develop, and flowing becomes a more instinctive way of life.

Consequently, when obstructions occur, you need to follow the practices for *losing* control explained throughout this book, including, of course, addressing your Personal Truths—particularly fear and resentment—and accepting "what is."

Be aware, though, that your initial successes can create their own anxieties, causing you to start pressing again. I learned this during the writing of this book. As I first began writing following the traumatic events I described in the introduction, important personal issues became clearer and clearer to me. I began to sort through the confusion and uncertainties in my life and better understood how things fit together. It literally felt as if I were making positive headway in putting together a thousand-piece puzzle. As this framework took shape and I found key pieces here and there, I became very excited. I experienced wonderful feelings I had never felt before. Remarkable insights came to me. I even benefited from reading initial drafts of chapters for guidance when I floundered, and this made me even more excited.

The honeymoon continued for about six months. Then I hit a dead end. I knew right away it wasn't writer's block but something far different. It was the realization that there were vital missing links—issues and challenges that I had not yet been able to resolve or even clarify. Simply put, the remaining pieces of my life puzzle did not fit. So I resorted to what I always did in such moments: I avidly pressed forward. I craved to learn what was eluding me—so much so, in fact, that I soon became depressed. At first, I refused to acknowledge my depression to myself, let alone others. I might admit only that I was feeling a "little low" as I desperately tried to escape my depression. Nothing worked. To the contrary, all my efforts made me feel worse, particularly considering that I was in the middle of writing a book about finding serenity.

Finally one day, I realized that I was not doing the very thing I had been strongly advocating: relinquishing control. To the contrary, I had been persisting and resisting. I also was not embracing my Personal Truths: fear and grief. I then gave myself "permission" to feel sad. Rather than further question or try to escape my "low tides," I tried to fully embrace my grief and accept that there was a greater purpose to my quagmire that I could not then comprehend. As I began to embrace my sadness and frustration, I felt more grounded. By the end of the next day, I felt much better. Better enough, in fact, to write some of these very pages.

I had learned an invaluable lesson: when you escape or withdraw—both forms of control—from unpleasant and unsettling feelings, you only prolong them. You must open your heart to life's low tides, for they are just as much a part of life's rhythm of truth as high tides are.

CREATING SYNERGY BY ACCEPTING "WHAT IS"

For many less fortunate, this task is even more challenging. Whether it is fate, bad luck, or reasons we cannot comprehend, some of us are dealt worse hands in life than others, be it serious illnesses, the loss of loved ones, financial deprivation, or even worse. An unfortunately common example is when responsible, loving parents have to endure the pain of children who have gone astray because of drugs or other addictions. I have heard such parents express many times that no matter what they did or how hard they tried to help their children get better, they could not prevent their children's downward slide. In fact, it only made their own lives more burdensome and stressful. Some of these parents also shared that it was only when they were able to accept that they were powerless over the situation and allowed their children to suffer (and learn from) the consequences of their destructive actions—even if that meant letting them live on the streets—were the parents' lives restored to normalcy. And in many but certainly not all cases, their wayward children eventually found the path back to health and safety on their own.

However great your misfortunes, the more you can accept the truth of your situation, the less the pain and discomfort will be. Thus, accepting "what is" enhances the ride in better times and softens the bumps in harder times.

What's exciting about the Wave is its synergistic impact on all aspects of your life. When you successfully apply it in one part of your life—work, for example—the positive energy and confidence carries over to other parts. The transition becomes almost automatic because of the inherent universality of the Wave. The synergistic momentum of this vital pendulum is one of the greatest thrills you will ever experience.

Riding the Wave makes your "whole" life more balanced, integrated, and enriched as you start enjoying the unplanned, spontaneous moments in life that are so special.

MOVING AHEAD

I HAVE COME TO realize something as I have better learned to apply the decontrol tools I write about: my urge to control never really ceases. It abates for varying periods, but it continues to surface—often without warning—particularly when triggered by my fear, anger, and anxiety. The important differences now are that I am much more aware of when and how I am being controlling and I have the means to quell the urge much sooner.

I am also more frequently enjoying the benefits that result from letting go of control when pursuing new opportunities and facing new challenges. In the past I would have obsessed and worried a lot and pressed for quick solutions. That now seldom happens. Instead, I view challenges as new learning opportunities. I try to be open-minded and patient and to trust that everything will work out in its own way, time, and place. And it usually does.

I encourage you, too, to apply the decontrol tools and techniques in my book that speak to you personally as you encounter new challenges in your life—particularly those that are uncertain, fearful, or overwhelming. Look at them as opportunities to expand your horizons and discard ways that no longer work for you.

As I have begun sharing and speaking about the benefits of giving up control, it has been especially rewarding that my message has resonated so strongly with people. I have found that so many people are ready to let go. Quite simply, they recognize that their controlling methods and devices haven't served them well, particularly in our increasingly complex world. I am heartened as people share their personal success stories with relinquishing control. I invite you to share your own stories, including what has worked for you—and what hasn't—by visiting my Decontrol Yourself blog at blog.losingcontrolfindingserenity.com.

Finally, although the idea of relinquishing control can at times seem unbearable or unfathomable, please let me assure you that it becomes much easier as you begin to experience the rewards that come when you let go. It may help if you think of and accept (as I do) life as being an ongoing, ever-changing mystery—a mystery that is clearly unsolvable yet one that reveals clues that can lead to significant life rewards IF you don't try solving the mystery.

ACKNOWLEDGMENTS

I WISH TO ACKNOWLEDGE and thank those who have played instrumental roles in the nearly twenty-five-year personal journey and exploration culminating in the publication of this book.

The first person I must thank is my beautiful (in every way) wife, Sigute, for being so supportive and encouraging throughout, including acting as my confidant and ad hoc advisor and proofreader. Thank you, sweetheart; I love you. Thank you, too, to my special children, Brandon, Lora, and Lana, whose independence and diverse personalities helped teach me the wisdom of letting go of parental control.

Thanks mucho to my fellow "Waver" Denis Kunstler, who shared some fun early rides with me. Thanks also to some supportive friends who encouraged and motivated me more than they may realize: Marcia Ross, Paul Henne, Norman Hull, Nijole Sparkis, Fritz Heede, Dave Kimball, Vic Kimball, and David Olsen.

A special thanks to my soulful friend Doris Wolz-Cohen for reviewing some early writings and sharing with me the importance of processing our "unwanted" feelings on an internal level as an essential means of reducing our external control responses. A special thanks as well to Jeff Brickell, a very supportive and intuitive life coach, who encouraged me to share my ideas and beliefs about control with others.

I am especially grateful to my fine team of highly talented and respected publishing professionals: Beth Lieberman, my line editor, thank you for your insightful suggestions for improving the manuscript and later polishing it in a manner that enhanced its flow and continuity; Dianne Woo, my copy editor, thank you for being so meticulous in ensuring that my writing was consistent and grammatically correct throughout; Mayapriya Long, thank you for lending your refined artistry to the book's cover and interior design; and a very special thanks to Sharon Goldinger, my experienced, trusted, and always professional "go to" publishing advisor, for always steering me in the right direction and to the right people.

And I would be remiss if I failed to acknowledge the important roles that my "adversaries" (real and perceived) played in helping shine light on the follies of my controlling misadventures and for helping me ultimately realize that "victory and success" are meaningful only when accompanied by a peaceful heart and mind.

Finally, I am forever grateful to the Alanon program and its guiding principles for confirming and enhancing my beliefs about the importance of letting go of control and to the members of its supportive fellowship for sharing their strength, hope, and experience.

ABOUT THE AUTHOR

Like most compulsive controllers, Daniel A. Miller was always driven to succeed. He graduated from UCLA with honors in business administration and finished in the top 5 percent of his class at the UCLA School of Law.

While still in his twenties, he became a popular real estate instructor in the UCLA extension program, and in his thirties he published a critically acclaimed, best-selling professional book, *How to Invest in Real Estate Syndicates*. He later founded the California Institute of Real Estate Education, which offered state-licensed seminars to thousands of real estate professionals.

Financial success came early to Danny. Celebrities and wealthy people entrusted him with large sums to invest on their behalf. By his midthirties he could afford to live in the exclusive Old Bel-Air section of Los Angeles, only a few doors away from Sylvester Stallone and just up the street from where Elvis Presley had once lived.

But for all his achievements and success, Danny had no sense of inner peace and serenity. He was imprisoned by his fears, anger, and anxieties and thus not open to the wonders all about him.

After a long series of personal setbacks, Danny finally began a new life journey based on letting go of control. He tried to go with the ups and downs and twists and turns of life, instead of resisting them and trying to control people and things.

He learned effective tools and techniques for *losing* control in important areas such as family, parenting, love and romance, the creative arts, sports, and the workplace. He became an accomplished fine artist, a published poet, a champion tournament tennis player, a happily married man, and a much wiser parent—all while cutting his work time by more than half.

Thus, through letting go of control, Danny found a different and more profound kind of success—an internal, core sense of well-being. He now counsels others and writes (on his blog at blog.losingcontrolfindingserenity.com) and speaks about the remarkable benefits of letting go of control. Please visit www.losingcontrolfindingserenity.com for keynote speaker information.

INDEX

Made in the USA
Columbia, SC
06 February 2023

11878083R00124